YOUR could ... in our next cookbook!

Share your tried & true family favorites with us instantly at

www.gooseberrypatch.com

If you'd rather jot 'em down by hand, just mail this form to...

Gooseberry Patch • Cookbooks – Call for Recipes
PO Box 812 • Columbus, OH 43216-0812

If your recipe is selected for a book, you'll receive a FREE copy!

Please share only your original recipes or those that you have made your own over the years.

Recipe Name:

Number of Servings:

Any fond memories about this recipe? Special touches you like to add or handy shortcuts?

Ingredients (include specific measurements):

Instructions (continue on back if needed):

Special Code: **cookbookspage**

Over ↗

Extra space for recipe if needed:

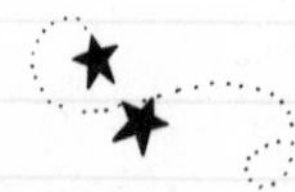

Tell us about yourself...

Your complete contact information is needed so that we can send you your FREE cookbook, if your recipe is published. Phone numbers and email addresses are kept private and will only be used if we have questions about your recipe.

Name:
Address:
City: State: Zip:
Email:
Daytime Phone:

Thank you! Vickie & Jo Ann

Quick & Easy
Recipes for Gatherings

More than 200 delicious recipes and clever tips to make any occasion extra special.

Gooseberry Patch

An imprint of Globe Pequot
246 Goose Lane
Guilford, CT 06437

www.gooseberrypatch.com

1•800•854•6673

 978-1-62093-408-1

Do you have a tried & true recipe...

tip, craft or memory that you'd like to see featured in a **Gooseberry Patch** cookbook? Visit our website at **www.gooseberrypatch.com** and follow the easy steps to submit your favorite family recipe. Or send them to us at:

Gooseberry Patch
PO Box 812
Columbus, OH 43216-0812

Don't forget to include the number of servings your recipe makes, plus your name, address, phone number and email address. If we select your recipe, your name will appear right along with it... and you'll receive a **FREE** copy of the book!

Contents

Dedication

To everyone who knows that scrumptious food makes any gathering special...but what really matters is the friendship we share!

Appreciation

A big thanks to all of you who shared your yummiest recipes for friendly get-togethers.

Dreamy Dips & Spreads

Quick & Easy Recipes for Gatherings

World's Best Cheese Ball

Laura Fredlund
Papillion, NE

This is my self-proclaimed world's best cheese ball. Try it and you might proclaim it too! Perfect for any friendly get-together. Serve with your favorite snack crackers.

8-oz. pkg. cream cheese, softened
5-oz. jar sharp pasteurized process cheese spread
1/4 c. crumbled blue cheese
2 to 3 green onions, diced
2 t. Worcestershire sauce
Garnish: chopped pecans

Combine cheeses, onions and Worcestershire sauce in a large bowl. Beat with an electric mixer on medium speed until well blended. Form into a ball and roll in chopped pecans. Place on a serving plate; chill until serving time. Serves 8.

A cheese ball, a basket of crackers and a bubbly beverage... it's party time! With any of the recipes in this chapter, you can easily get the party started.

Dreamy Dips & Spreads

Chicken Enchilada Dip

Lanita Anderson
Chesapeake, VA

Great for game day! I tasted this recipe at a Navy Chaplains' Wives function and just had to have the recipe. It's a hearty appetizer that you could easily make a meal of. If you like it hot and spicy, add a couple tablespoons of chopped jalapeños. Serve with tortilla chips.

2 boneless, skinless chicken breasts, cooked and diced
8-oz. pkg. cream cheese, softened
1 c. mayonnaise
4-oz. can diced green chiles
8-oz. pkg. shredded Cheddar cheese

In a bowl, combine all ingredients except shredded cheese; mix well. Spread in a lightly greased 2-quart casserole dish; top with shredded cheese. Bake, uncovered, at 350 degrees for 35 to 45 minutes, until hot and bubbly. Serves 8 to 10.

Fresh Chili-Cheese Dip

April Jacobs
Loveland, CO

Made with garden-fresh tomatoes and peppers...tortilla chips never had it so good! It's ready to serve in a jiffy.

16-oz. pkg. pasteurized process cheese, cubed
3 T. milk
1 c. ripe tomatoes, diced
2 to 3 jalapeño peppers, seeded and diced
1/4 to 1/2 t. hot pepper sauce

In a saucepan over low heat, combine cheese and milk. Cook, stirring constantly, until melted and smooth. Stir in tomatoes, peppers and hot sauce; heat through. Serve warm. Makes 8 servings.

Slow cookers are perfect serving helpers! Just plug them in and they'll keep hot dips bubbly and yummy with no effort at all.

Quick & Easy
Recipes for Gatherings

Busy Mom's Oh-So-Good Party Dip

Lisa Childers
Hopkinsville, KY

People are amazed at how tasty this simple and attractive dip is! This recipe is always a favorite, and there are hardly ever any leftovers. Great for parties and barbecues, or as a holiday appetizer.

16-oz. container sour cream
16-oz. container small-curd cottage cheese
1.4-oz. pkg. vegetable soup mix
1 bunch green onions, diced
1 green pepper, diced
1 tomato, diced
8-oz. pkg. finely shredded Cheddar cheese
round buttery crackers

In a shallow serving bowl, mix together sour cream, cottage cheese, soup mix and onions; spread evenly in bottom of bowl. Layer with green pepper, tomato and shredded cheese in the order listed; do not mix. Cover and refrigerate for at least one hour to overnight, to allow flavors to blend. Serve chilled with crackers. Serves 12 to 14.

Blanching makes fresh-cut veggies crisp and bright...super for dipping. Bring a large pot of salted water to a rolling boil, add trimmed veggies and boil for 3 to 4 minutes, just until they begin to soften. Immediately remove veggies to a bowl of ice water. Cool, drain and pat dry.

Dreamy Dips & Spreads

Havarti Dill Cheese Ball

Shirley Howie
Foxboro, MA

I brought this yummy cheese ball to a recent neighborhood gathering and it was a big hit! Serve with assorted crackers.

8-oz. pkg. cream cheese, softened
1/2 c. shredded Havarti cheese
1/3 c. crumbled feta cheese
1 T. milk
1-1/2 t. dried dill weed
2 green onions, finely chopped
1/3 c. slivered almonds, toasted and chopped

In a large bowl, combine all ingredients except almonds. Beat with an electric mixer on low speed until blended. Beat on medium speed until fluffy. Cover and refrigerate at least 2 hours, until firm enough to hold together. Just before serving, shape cheese mixture into a ball; roll in almonds. Serves 12 to 15.

A quick and tasty appetizer in an instant...place a block of cream cheese on a serving plate, spoon sweet-hot pepper jelly over it and serve with crisp crackers. Works great with fruit chutney or spicy salsa too!

Texas Caviar

Elizabeth Smithson
Mayfield, KY

I make this often! Everyone is surprised by the results and asks for the recipe. Serve with tortilla chips and mini sweet peppers for dipping.

- 15-1/2 oz. can black beans, drained
- 15-1/4 oz. can corn, drained and liquid reserved
- 1/2 c. red pepper, chopped
- 1/2 c. green onion, sliced
- 1/2 c. favorite salsa
- 1/2 c. fresh cilantro, snipped
- 1 clove garlic, minced
- 1-oz. pkg. Italian salad dressing mix
- 1 T. lime juice
- 1 t. dried oregano

In a large serving bowl, combine all ingredients except reserved corn liquid. Toss to mix well; add a little of the reserved liquid, to desired consistency. Cover and refrigerate for 2 hours before serving. Makes 12 to 15 servings.

For an instant chip & dip set, fill a wine glass or tumbler with dip, set it in a bowl and surround with chips.

Dreamy Dips & Spreads

Fresh Avocado Dip

Gretchen Brown
Hillsboro, OR

This recipe is so simple, yet delicious. It is best to chill it for a couple of hours so that the flavors blend together. Serve with tortilla chips.

2 15-oz. cans black-eyed peas, rinsed and drained
2 11-oz. cans white shoepeg corn, rinsed and drained
2 10-oz. cans diced tomatoes with green chiles, drained
2 avocados, peeled, pitted and diced
1/2 c. red onion, diced
3/4 c. zesty Italian salad dressing
2 T. lime juice
1/2 t. salt

Combine all ingredients in a large bowl; stir gently to mix. Cover and chill, if desired. Makes 8 to 10 servings.

Dress up dips and spreads with a simple garnish. Reserve some of the chopped vegetables in the recipe to sprinkle on top...add a toss of chopped fresh parsley or pimento to a light-colored creamy dip.

Mrs. B's Shrimp Cheese Ball

Joyce Sipe
New Wilmington, PA

This is a yummy recipe that I got from my boss's wife. She had studied to be a home economic teacher and was a wonderful cook.

8-oz. pkg. cream cheese, softened
3-oz. pkg. cream cheese, softened
1 lb. frozen small cooked, peeled shrimp, thawed and coarsely chopped
17 green and/or black olives, thinly sliced
3 T. mayonnaise
2 T. onion, minced
1 T. dried parsley
Garnish: chopped walnuts or pecans
assorted snack crackers

In a large bowl, blend together all ingredients except garnish and crackers. Cover and refrigerate for several hours. Shape into a ball; cover and chill again. At serving time, roll in chopped nuts. Set on a serving plate and surround with a variety of crackers. Serves 20.

Place a copy of your guest list near the phone so you can check off replies. If anyone has forgotten to call by the reply date, give them a call so you'll be sure to have plenty of refreshments for everyone.

Dreamy Dips & Spreads

Jan's Hot Crab Dip

Jan Purnell
Littlestown, PA

Hands down, this is the most requested of my recipes for parties and family get-togethers. It always pleases! Serve with snack crackers, pita chips or slices of French bread.

8-oz. pkg. lump crabmeat
8-oz. pkg. cream cheese, softened
1/2 c. sour cream
2 T. mayonnaise-style salad dressing or mayonnaise
1 T. lemon juice
1-1/4 t. Worcestershire sauce
2 t. seafood seasoning
1/2 t. dry mustard
1/8 t. garlic salt
1 T. milk
1/4 c. shredded Cheddar cheese, divided

Pick over crabmeat for shells; set aside. In a large bowl, combine remaining ingredients except milk and shredded cheese; stir until smooth. Add enough milk to make a creamy consistency. Stir in 2 tablespoons shredded cheese. Fold crabmeat into cream cheese mixture. Spoon into a lightly greased one-quart casserole dish; top with remaining cheese. Bake, uncovered, at 325 degrees for about 45 minutes, until bubbly and golden. Makes 16 servings.

A dip buffet will be fun at your next get-together! Have plenty of chips, crackers, sliced veggies, baguette rounds and pita triangles on hand. Get creative and serve your dips in unexpected containers such as hollowed-out vegetables and breads.

3-Cheese Spinach & Artichoke Dip

JoAnn
Gooseberry Patch

My family can't resist this warm, creamy slow-cooker dip! We love it with toasted baguette slices or white corn tortilla chips.

1 c. mushrooms, chopped
1 T. butter
2 cloves garlic, minced
8-oz. pkg. cream cheese, softened
1-1/2 c. mayonnaise
1 c. plus 2 T. grated Parmesan cheese, divided
1 c. shredded mozzarella cheese, divided
14-oz. can artichoke hearts, drained and chopped
10-oz. pkg. frozen chopped spinach, thawed and squeezed dry
1/4 c. red pepper, diced

In a skillet over medium heat, cook mushrooms in butter until tender. Add garlic; cook for one minute and remove from heat. In a large bowl, combine cream cheese, mayonnaise, one cup Parmesan cheese and 3/4 cup mozzarella cheese. Stir in mushroom mixture, artichokes, spinach and red pepper. Spoon into a 3-quart slow cooker; sprinkle with remaining cheeses. Cover and cook on low setting for 2 to 3 hours, until bubbly and cheeses are melted. Makes 4 cups.

Whenever a guest asks, "How can I help?" be ready with an answer! Whether it's setting the table, filling glasses with ice or even bringing their special dessert, friends are always happy to pitch in.

The Best Blue Cheese Ball

Debra Arch
Kewanee, IL

Beware! If you start eating this cheese ball with crackers, you won't be able to stop! This recipe makes two balls and freezes well...on the rare chance there is one left! We love it with round buttery crackers.

2 8-oz. pkgs. cream cheese, softened
5-oz. container crumbled blue or Gorgonzola cheese
1/2 c. green olives with pimentos, chopped
2-oz. pkg dried beef, chopped
1-oz. pkg. ranch salad dressing mix
2 T. mayonnaise-style salad dressing
1 c. pecans, finely chopped

In a large bowl, combine all ingredients except pecans. Use an electric mixer on medium speed to blend well. Divide mixture in half; form into 2 balls and roll in chopped pecans. Wrap in plastic wrap and refrigerate for 8 hours, or overnight. Best when made the day before serving. Makes 12 servings.

Single servings! Roll a favorite cheese ball mixture into bite-size mini balls and place in paper muffin cups. Fill more paper muffin cups with crackers and pretzels and arrange alongside mini cheese balls... guests can enjoy one of each.

Ann's White Queso Dip

Ann Tober
Biscoe, AR

We love this cheesy dip on tacos and enchiladas...of course, it's great with tortilla chips too!

1-1/2 t. olive oil
1/4 c. sweet onion, finely chopped
1/2 to 1 jalapeño pepper, minced and seeds removed to taste
16-oz. pkg. shredded white American cheese
1 c. milk
1/4 to 1/2 c. low-sodium chicken broth
1/2 c. ripe tomato, finely diced
1/4 c. fresh cilantro, chopped

Heat oil in a large saucepan over medium-low heat. Add onion and jalapeño; cook for 2 to 3 minutes. Reduce heat to low. Add cheese and milk; cook and stir until smooth and cheese is melted. Stir in broth to desired consistency; add tomato and cilantro. Cook for one minute; serve warm. Serves 6.

Jack Cheese Chile Dip

Ruth Thomas
Muncie, IN

Our friends and we used to enjoy this easy dip just about every weekend while we watched a movie or played cards together. It's delicious with tortilla chips, potato chips and snack crackers.

14-1/2 oz. can stewed tomatoes, drained
3 to 4 green onions, finely chopped
4-oz. can diced green chiles
8-oz. pkg. shredded Monterey Jack cheese

Mix together all ingredients in a serving bowl, breaking up tomatoes with your hands. Cover and refrigerate for several hours. Serve chilled. Makes 4 to 5 servings.

A person who can bring the spirit of laughter into a room is indeed blessed.

– Bennett Cerf

Dreamy Dips & Spreads

Chicken Ranch Dip

Tina Matie
Alma, GA

This is a recipe that my family loves. We always make this for our Christmas get-together. It's really good with scoop-type tortilla chips, to scoop up every delicious bit!

8-oz. pkg. cream cheese, softened
24-oz. bottle ranch salad dressing
3 13-oz. cans chicken breast, drained and flaked
1/2 to 1 6-oz. bottle hot pepper sauce, to taste
8-oz. pkg. shredded Monterey Jack cheese
8-oz. pkg. shredded Pepper Jack cheese

In a large bowl, blend together cream cheese and salad dressing; set aside. Spread chicken in a lightly greased 13"x9" baking pan. Sprinkle chicken with hot sauce; spread cream cheese mixture over top. Sprinkle shredded cheeses on top. Bake, uncovered, at 350 degrees for 20 to 25 minutes, until bubbly. Makes 10 to 12 servings.

Yvonne's Chili Dip

Betty Kozlowski
Newnan, GA

This disappears quickly...my whole family loves this dip! The first time I tried it at a church potluck, I knew I had to get the recipe from Yvonne. She raised four boys and was used to providing hearty meals for them. Serve with scoop-type tortilla chips or corn chips.

2 8-oz. pkgs. low-fat cream cheese, softened
20-oz. can chili, no beans
2 lbs. ground turkey or beef, browned and drained
3 c. shredded Cheddar cheese

Spread softened cream cheese in the bottom of an ungreased 13"x9" baking pan; set aside. Mix chili and cooked turkey or beef; spread over cream cheese. Top with shredded cheese. Bake, uncovered, at 350 degrees for 15 minutes, or microwave for 5 minutes, until cheese melts. Serve hot. Serves 12.

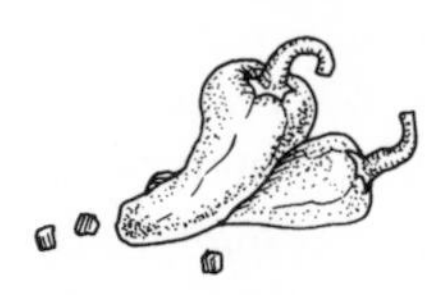

Cold Cucumber Salsa

Anne Alesauskas
Minocqua, WI

On one of the hottest days of the year, I was a guest at a dinner party. One of the appetizers was similar to this and it was amazing! I just knew I had to try to recreate it, so here you are...my take on cucumber salsa, a refreshing, healthy summer snack. Serve with tortilla chips or toasted baguette slices.

2 c. cucumbers, peeled, seeded and finely chopped
1/2 c. ripe tomato, finely chopped
1/4 c. red onion, finely diced
2 T. jalapeño pepper, or to taste, chopped
2 T. fresh cilantro, finely minced
1 clove garlic, minced
1/4 c. fat-free sour cream or plain yogurt
1-1/2 t. lime juice
1 t. lemon juice
1/8 t. ground cumin
salt and pepper to taste

In a small bowl, mix together vegetables, cilantro and garlic; set aside. In another small bowl, combine remaining ingredients; pour sparingly over cucumber mixture. Cover and chill. As salsa stands, cucumbers will give off liquid. More of the dressing may be added if needed, but add it slowly at first, so it doesn't get too runny. Serves 6.

When the weather is nice, take the food & festivities outdoors to the backyard. You'll be making memories together...and just about everything tastes even better outdoors!

Easy Garlic Hummus

Courtney Stultz
Weir, KS

We are big-time snackers at our house! Honestly, sometimes we replace our typical lunch with a spread of snacks like dips, veggies and fruits. Hummus is one of our favorite dips and it is so easy to make. Seriously, it takes me longer to wash the food processor after making it than to actually toss it together!

15-oz. can garbanzo beans, drained and rinsed
juice of 1 large lemon
2 T. olive oil
2 T. tahini
4 cloves garlic, roasted if possible
1/2 t. ground cumin
1 t. sea salt
Garnish: paprika, chopped fresh parsley
sliced vegetables or crackers

In a food processor or high-powered blender, combine beans, lemon juice, olive oil, tahini, garlic, cumin and salt. Blend on high for about 2 to 4 minutes, to desired consistency. Transfer hummus to a serving bowl; sprinkle with paprika and parsley. Serve with an assortment of sliced vegetables or crackers. Serves 8.

"Everything bagel" spice is great for jazzing up creamy dips, pita chips, potato skins...you name it! Mix up your own by filling a jar with 2 teaspoons coarse salt and one tablespoon each of poppy seed, toasted sesame seed, dried minced garlic and dried minced onion. Yum!

Marta's Cream Cheese Ball

Marta Norton
Redlands, CA

I discovered this recipe in the 1980s and it quickly became my most-requested dish for family gatherings. Whether served with Melba toast and round buttery crackers, or veggies like carrot and celery sticks, it's sure to be a hit!

2 8-oz. pkgs. cream cheese, softened
1 c. cooked ham, finely chopped
1/2 c. mayonnaise
1 t. onion, finely diced
1/2 t. dry mustard
Optional: 1/2 t. dried parsley
2 c. pecans, finely chopped

Combine all ingredients except pecans in a large bowl; mix well. Cover and refrigerate at least 6 hours or overnight, up to 2 days. Dip will set up. To serve, form cheese mixture into one large ball or 2 smaller balls; roll in pecans and set on a serving plate. Serves 8 to 10.

Pineapple-Cream Cheese Spread

Beckie Apple
Grannis, AR

This a favorite make-ahead spread that's welcome at any occasion. It keeps refrigerated up to 2 weeks...very handy at busy times! Serve with crisp crackers or spread on toasted bread.

8-oz. pkg. cream cheese, softened
15-1/4 oz. can crushed pineapple, well drained
3 to 4 T. creamy horseradish sauce, to taste
1-1/2 c. finely shredded Cheddar cheese
crisp crackers or toasted bread slices

Cut cream cheese block into 4 parts. Place in a microwave-safe bowl and microwave for one minute. Remove from microwave; beat with a spoon until creamy. Add pineapple and horseradish; stir well. Blend in shredded cheese. Cover and refrigerate for one to 2 hours, or up to 2 weeks. Serves 8 to 10.

Mary's B-L-T Dip

Mary Richmond
Weymouth, MA

This is an easy dip recipe I found on a package years ago. Whenever I serve it, I get plenty of compliments on how tasty it is. Try it and see for yourself!

8-oz. container sour cream
8-oz. jar mayonnaise
3 plum tomatoes, diced and drained
1/2 c. real bacon bits
Garnish: romaine lettuce leaves
crackers, corn chip scoops or sliced vegetables

In a bowl, combine sour cream and mayonnaise. Fold in tomatoes and bacon bits. Cover and chill thoroughly. To serve, arrange lettuce leaves on a serving plate; scoop dip into the center. Surround with crackers, chips or vegetables. Serves 10 to 12.

Party Chicken Spread

Candice Winters
Jacksonville, IL

This spread is delicious on crackers. I have made this for years now, and everyone loves it. It's just a little different. Whenever I take it to a get-together, everyone requests the recipe!

6 4-1/4 oz. cans white meat chicken spread
8-oz. pkg. cream cheese, softened
3 T. mayonnaise
2 T. onion, finely chopped
2 T. soy sauce, or more to taste

Combine all ingredients in a large bowl; stir until thoroughly mixed. Cover and refrigerate for at least 3 to 4 hours. Makes about 3 cups.

Make your own crunchy baguette crisps. Thinly slice a French loaf... prettiest on the diagonal. Arrange slices on a baking sheet. Sprinkle with olive oil and garlic powder, then bake at 400 degrees for 12 to 15 minutes.

Olive Tapenade

Joan Chance
Houston, TX

A great spread for crackers or toasted bread. I even like it in a sandwich! Serve with crackers, flatbread, baguette, or slices of a toasted artisan bread. It is vegetarian or vegan.

1/2 c. black olives, drained
1/2 c. green olives, drained
2 cloves garlic, chopped
Optional: 1 T. capers, drained
2 T. olive oil
1 t. lemon juice
1/4 t. pepper, or to taste

Combine all ingredients in a food processor. Process for a few seconds, until chopped but not too smooth. If you don't have a food processor, use a sharp knife to finely mince olives and garlic. Combine with remaining ingredients and mix well. Cover and chill until serving time. Serves 6 to 8.

Spoon some creamy vegetable dip into a wide plastic cup and add crunchy celery and carrot sticks and red pepper strips. Easy to snack and go!

Roasted Garlic Spread

Margaret Callam
Georgetown, IN

This is a delicious appetizer. It's not only a family favorite, but a crowd-pleaser as well. The garlic mellows as it cooks. Great for a holiday gathering, football tailgate or a company potluck.

4 whole heads garlic
1/4 c. extra-virgin olive oil
2 8-oz. pkgs. cream cheese, softened
1/2 c. butter, softened
1 t. salt
1/4 c. fresh chives, minced
sliced French bread, warmed

Cut the tops off garlic heads, leaving heads intact. Arrange heads in a small casserole dish; drizzle with olive oil. Cover with aluminum foil. Bake at 350 degrees for 45 minutes. Uncover and bake an additional 10 minutes, or until garlic is soft. Remove from oven; cool completely. When garlic heads are cool, remove and discard outermost layers of the papery skin. Scoop out soft garlic pulp with a small spoon and set aside. Beat cream cheese and butter with an electric mixer on high speed until light and fluffy. Add garlic pulp and salt; beat again until blended. Stir in chives. Serve spread over warm slices of French bread. May keep refrigerated up to 2 weeks. Makes 2-1/2 cups.

Set out bowls of nuts in the shell for a quick snack that will keep early-arriving guests busy while you put the finishing touches on the dinner table. Don't forget the nutcracker!

Y'All Come Pimento Cheese

Karen Antonides
Gahanna, OH

My daughter moved from Ohio to North Carolina, and through our travels visiting her, we have enjoyed the southern cuisine we have encountered. We love pimento cheese served with crackers or baguettes. This is a wonderful basic dip that is so versatile that you can make it as mild or spicy as you wish, with the addition of chopped jalapeños or smoked paprika.

8-oz. pkg. finely shredded sharp Cheddar cheese
1/3 to 1/2 c. mayonnaise
2 t. Dijon mustard
1/4 t. garlic powder
1/4 t. onion powder
1/4 t. cayenne pepper
4-oz. jar diced pimentos, well drained
Optional: 1/4 c. green olives, finely chopped
crackers or baguettes

Place cheese in a large bowl; set aside. In another bowl, mix together mayonnaise, mustard and seasonings. Add to cheese; mix well. Add pimentos and olives, if desired; mix well. Cover and refrigerate. Best made a day ahead, to allow flavors to blend. Serve with crackers or baguettes. Serves 15 to 20.

Guests will love these veggie dippers. Thread carrot and celery slices, cauliflower and broccoli flowerets and jumbo olives onto small wooden skewers in different combinations. Arrange around yummy dips and enjoy!

Warm Pepperoni Dip

Lori Broderick
Plattsburg, MO

Whenever I bring this delicious dip to a get-together, I'm always asked for the recipe. It's different and very yummy. Serve with tortilla chips, crackers or sliced veggies.

- 2 8-oz. pkgs. cream cheese, softened
- 8-oz. container sour cream
- 1/4 to 1/2 c. green pepper, diced
- 5-oz. pkg. sliced pepperoni, or to taste, diced
- 1/4 t. garlic powder
- 2.8-oz. can French fried onions, divided

Combine all ingredients except onions in a bowl; blend well. Stir in 1/2 can of onions. Spread in an ungreased one-quart casserole dish. Bake, uncovered, at 350 degrees for 20 minutes; top with remaining onions the last 5 minutes of baking. Serve warm. Makes 10 servings.

For guests who are eating light, reduced-fat shredded cheese, sour cream and cream cheese are an easy substitute for their full-fat counterparts in recipes. Flavor and texture may vary from brand to brand...you're sure to find some that you like just as much as the "real thing."

Baked Crab Dip

Leona Krivda
Belle Vernon, PA

This tasty dip has been well liked by all of my guests. Serve with chips, crackers, bread slices or veggies.

8-oz. pkg. cream cheese, softened
1 c. mayonnaise
1/2 c. grated Parmesan cheese
4 green onions, sliced
2 t. Worcestershire sauce
2 t. lemon juice
1/2 t. cracked pepper
6-1/2 oz. can lump crabmeat, drained and flaked

Combine all ingredients except crabmeat in a bowl; mix well. Gently fold in crabmeat until well combined. Transfer to a lightly greased one-quart casserole dish. Bake, uncovered, at 375 degrees for 35 to 45 minutes, until golden. Remove from oven; let cool for 20 minutes before serving. Serves 8 to 10.

Creamy Clam Dip

John Alexander
New Britain, CT

Reminds us of days at the seashore! Serve with your favorite kettle potato chips or white tortilla chips.

8-oz. pkg. cream cheese, softened
6-1/2 oz. can minced clams, drained and juice reserved
juice of 1/2 lemon
1 t. Worcestershire sauce
2 green onions, minced
1 to 2 drops hot pepper sauce

In a bowl, mash cream cheese with a fork until soft and creamy. Add one tablespoon reserved clam juice; blend well. Stir in lemon juice and Worcestershire sauce; fold in clams, onions and hot sauce. If dip is too thick, stir in a little of remaining clam juice to desired consistency. Cover and chill up to 2 days before serving. Makes 1-1/2 cups.

Colorful new plastic pails make whimsical servers for chips and snacks.

Dreamy Dips & Spreads

Savory Salmon Ball

Gladys Brehm
Quakertown, PA

An easy dip appetizer for the holidays...or just to make any day more special! Great with snack crackers, or carrot and celery sticks as well as bite-size broccoli and cauliflower flowerets.

8-oz. pkg. cream cheese, room temperature
14-3/4 oz. can salmon, drained and flaked
2 T. onion, grated
1 T. lemon juice
1 t. prepared horseradish
1/4 t. salt
3 drops smoke-flavored cooking sauce

Place cream cheese in a large bowl; stir until smooth. Add remaining ingredients and mix thoroughly. Cover and refrigerate at least 4 hours, or overnight. Uncover and form mixture into a ball. Wrap in plastic wrap; return to refrigerator until serving time. Serves 15.

A great make-ahead tip! Give cheese balls plenty of chilling time before rolling in chopped nuts, herbs or other coatings...at least a few hours, or up to 5 days ahead of time. Add the crunchy coating just before serving.

Awesome Hot Taco Dip

Stephanie Dardani-D'Esposito
Ravena, NY

My daughters love this taco dip. It's best hot out of the oven... so gooey and delicious! We like it with corn chips or tortilla chips.

16-oz. can refried beans
1-1/4 oz. pkg. taco seasoning mix
8-oz. pkg. cream cheese, softened
16-oz. container sour cream
16-oz. jar favorite salsa
8-oz. pkg. shredded Cheddar cheese
Garnish: shredded lettuce, sliced black olives and green onions

In a bowl, mix together beans and seasoning mix. Spread in the bottom of a lightly greased 13"x9" baking pan; set aside. In another bowl, blend cream cheese and sour cream; spread over bean mixture. Pour salsa evenly over all; top with shredded cheese. Bake, uncovered, at 350 degrees for 20 minutes, or until hot and bubbly. At serving time, top with lettuce, olives and onions. Makes 8 servings.

Try serving "light" dippers with hearty full-flavored dips and spreads. Fresh veggies, pita wedges, baked tortilla chips and multi-grain crispbread are all sturdy enough to scoop, yet won't overshadow the flavor of the dip.

Dreamy Dips & Spreads

Garden-Fresh Salsa

Vickie
Gooseberry Patch

We love this fresh and easy salsa. Serve with scoop-type tortilla chips to get every bit! Great on tacos too.

- 28-oz. can petite diced tomatoes
- 2 zucchini, finely chopped
- 1 c. red onion, chopped
- 1/3 c. fresh cilantro, chopped
- 1 jalapeño pepper, seeded and chopped
- 2 cloves garlic, minced
- 2 T. lemon juice
- pepper to taste

In a large bowl, combine tomatoes with juice and remaining ingredients; mix well. Cover and refrigerate for 2 hours to allow flavors to blend. Makes 3 cups.

Best Veggie Dip

Barb Bargdill
Gooseberry Patch

This creamy, herby dip will feed lots of hungry folks! Serve with a big platter of colorful veggies.

- 16-oz. container sour cream
- 16-oz. jar mayonnaise
- 1 T. dried, minced onion
- 1 T. dried parsley
- 1/2 t. dried dill weed
- 2 t. seasoned salt
- 1/2 t. Worcestershire sauce
- 3 to 4 drops hot pepper sauce

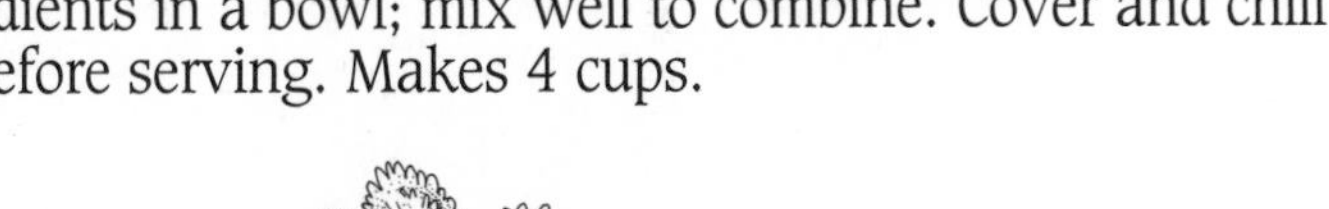

Combine all ingredients in a bowl; mix well to combine. Cover and chill at least 2 hours before serving. Makes 4 cups.

Fresh cilantro...you either love it or hate it! If you're in the latter group, fresh parsley makes a fine substitute for some or all of the cilantro in a recipe.

Easy Guacamole

Krista Marshall
Fort Wayne, IN

Guacamole is one of my favorite dips...I can even make a meal out of it! So this easy version is great for a quick lunch. Serve with tortilla chips or your favorite snack crackers.

2 avocados, peeled, pitted and chopped
1/4 tomato, chopped
2 T. onion, chopped
2 T. olive oil
juice of 1/2 lemon
1/2 t. kosher salt
pepper to taste

Place avocados in a bowl; mash to desired consistency using a potato masher or a fork. Add remaining ingredients; mix all together. For the best flavor, cover and chill for one hour before serving. Serves 4 to 6.

To tell if an avocado is ripe, gently press at the pointy end. If it gives, it's ripe! If it's still a bit firm, place in a paper bag at room temperature until softened.

Dreamy Dips & Spreads

Slow-Cooker Cheese Dip

LaDeana Cooper
Batavia, OH

Tailgating, reunions, holidays...oh my! This is great for any kind of get-together. It's the first dish to be emptied every time! I set the temp control on warm and serve with chips and fresh veggies to dip.

16-oz. pkg. mild ground pork sausage, browned and well drained
16-oz. pkg. pasteurized process cheese, cut into 1-inch cubes
1 c. favorite salsa
hot pepper sauce to taste

Combine all ingredients in a 5-quart slow cooker. Cover and cook on low setting for 2 hours, or on high setting for one hour, until cheese melts. Stir before serving. Serves 10.

Layered Salsa Dip

Julie Warren
Valdosta, GA

My family has enjoyed this yummy dip for years. It's so quick & easy. It's very showy to take to an event too. Serve with your favorite crunchy corn chips.

8-oz. pkg. sour cream, softened
1 c. favorite mild, medium or hot salsa
1 c. shredded Cheddar or Cheddar Jack cheese
Optional: chopped green onions or fresh parsley

Spread sour cream in a square or rectangular serving dish; spread salsa over sour cream layer. Sprinkle shredded cheese evenly over salsa. Garnish with chopped green onions or parsley, if desired. Cover and chill until serving time. Makes 6 to 8 servings.

Shred a block of cheese in a jiffy. Freeze wrapped cheese for 10 to 20 minutes...it will just glide across the grater!

Fiesta Time Salsa

Geneva Rogers
Gillette, WY

This salsa is a must-have at our family parties and barbecues. It's great with homemade corn chips and also wonderful on tacos and even eggs. Depending on what we are making it for, sometimes we purée it and other times we make it chunky. I like to use fresh jalapeños from my garden. Feel free to add more jalapeños if you like more heat.

1 to 2 jalapeño peppers, seeded and chopped
1/4 c. onion, diced
14-1/2 oz. can diced tomatoes with green chiles
14-1/2 oz. can peeled whole tomatoes
3/4 t. garlic salt
1/2 t. ground cumin
1/4 t. sugar

Combine jalapeños and onion in a food processor; process for a few seconds. Add both cans of tomatoes with juice, seasonings and sugar; process to desired consistency. Transfer to a covered container; chill for at least 2 hours or overnight. Makes 6 servings.

Is your dinner table big enough for just a few guests? No worries! Just make sure the food you serve can be held in one hand and eaten with a spoon or fork. Sandwiches with chips and salsa followed by brownies would be great.

Strawberry-Pineapple Salsa

Stephanie Mayer
Portsmouth, VA

My family enjoys this fresh fruity, spicy salsa with white tortilla chips or cinnamon pita chips. It's great on grilled chicken too. If you're not serving it for a few hours, stir in the strawberries at the last minute, so they don't tint the pineapple pink.

1 lb. strawberries, hulled and chopped
1/2 pineapple, peeled, cored and chopped
1/4 c. red onion, finely chopped
2 T. fresh cilantro, chopped
1 T. fresh mint, chopped
1 jalapeño or serrano pepper, seeded and minced
2 T. lime juice
1 t. lime zest
1 T. olive oil
1/4 t. salt

Combine all ingredients in a large bowl; stir gently to mix. Cover and chill until serving time. Serves 10 to 12.

Make your own cinnamon-sugar tortilla chips. Brush 6 flour tortillas with oil on both sides. Mix one cup sugar and one tablespoon cinnamon in a shallow bowl. Coat chips well and cut into wedges or strips. Bake at 425 degrees for 8 to 10 minutes, turning once or twice, until crisp and golden. Delicious with fruit dips!

Piña Colada Dip

Lynda McCormick
Burkburnett, TX

A great summertime treat! Enjoy this scrumptious dip at your next family cookout or while watching your favorite movie together. Sliced seasonal fruit and cubed angel food or pound cake make delicious dippers.

2 8-oz. containers low-fat plain yogurt
3.4-oz. pkg. instant vanilla pudding mix
1 c. crushed pineapple, drained
1 t. coconut extract
1 t. rum extract
1 c. frozen whipped topping, thawed

In a bowl, blend yogurt and dry pudding mix; stir in pineapple and extracts. Fold in whipped topping. Cover and refrigerate until serving time. Makes 2-1/2 cups.

For cute take-home gifts, fill mini Mason jars with a favorite homemade dip or spread. Tie on a recipe card and a spreader with a bit of ribbon...guests will love it!

Brownie Batter Dip

Kerry Mayer
Dunham Springs, LA

Is it an appetizer? Is it dessert? We don't know, but we don't care... we all love it! Delicious with pretzel twists and sliced apples.

1/2 c. butter, melted
2/3 c. sugar
1/3 c. baking cocoa
1/2 c. all-purpose flour
1/4 t. salt
1/2 c. plain Greek yogurt
Garnish: candy sprinkles or mini candy-coated chocolates

In a bowl, whisk together melted butter and sugar until well mixed. Stir in baking cocoa, flour and salt. Fold in yogurt, stirring until smooth. Cover and chill. Just before serving, top with desired garnish. Makes 2-1/2 cups.

Use tiered cake stands to serve dippers and bite-size appetizers... so handy, and they take up less space on the buffet table.

Paula's Pineapple Cheese Ball

Hailey Farrar
San Luis Obispo, CA

My mom Paula is famous for this recipe. The recipe actually originated with my grandmother Erma, who made it for my mom's baby shower when she was expecting my oldest sister. Our family has been making it for over 35 years now. It's always requested when we're invited to a holiday gathering...it just isn't the same without this cheese ball!

2 8-oz. pkgs. cream cheese, softened
8-oz. can crushed pineapple, drained
1/4 c. green onions, chopped
2 T. onion, chopped
1 T. seasoned salt
1 c. chopped pecans, divided
thin wheat crackers, buttery club crackers

In a bowl, mix together all ingredients except 1/4 cup pecans and crackers. Cover and chill for one hour to overnight. Shape into a ball; roll in pecans and chill again. Makes 2 small cheese balls or one large one. Serve with crackers. Makes 15 to 20 servings.

For tasty fun at your next game-day gathering, turn any favorite cheese ball recipe into a football. Just shape, sprinkle with paprika and pipe on sour cream or cream cheese "laces"...so easy!

Dreamy Dips & Spreads

Pecan Cranberry Spread

Marsha Baker
Pioneer, OH

This simple dip tastes so good and is perfect for any friendly gathering. I love the tasty combo of cranberry and orange. This can be made several days ahead before serving. Serve with crackers.

8-oz. pkg. cream cheese, softened
1/2 c. sweetened dried cranberries
1/2 c. chopped pecans
1/4 c. frozen orange juice concentrate, thawed
Optional: 1/2 t. cinnamon

In a bowl, beat cream cheese with an electric mixer on medium-low speed until soft and fluffy. Add remaining ingredients; stir to combine. Cover with plastic wrap and refrigerate until flavors blend, at least one hour. Makes 5 to 6 servings.

Slow-Cooked Brie

Zoe Bennett
Columbia, SC

A scrumptious snack with no effort at all! Serve with apple slices and toasted baguette slices.

8-oz. pkg. round brie cheese, unwrapped
1/4 c. sweetened dried cranberries, chopped
1/3 c. candied or toasted pecans, chopped

Trim and discard rind from top of cheese; place cheese in a small slow cooker. Top with cranberries and pecans. Cover and cook on slow setting for 3 to 4 hours, or on high setting for 2 hours, until cheese is very soft. Serve warm. Makes 8 servings.

May our house always be too small to hold all of our friends.

– Myrtle Reed

Chocolate Chip Cheese Ball

Becky Butler
Keller, TX

This is not only easy to prepare, but so much fun to eat! Perfect for a bridal shower or Girls' Night In...any gathering with people of all ages will love this treat.

8-oz. pkg. cream cheese, softened
1/2 c. butter, softened
1/2 c. pecans, finely chopped
2 T. light brown sugar, packed
3/4 c. powdered sugar
1 t. vanilla extract
3/4 c. mini semi-sweet chocolate chips
vanilla wafers, gingersnaps or graham crackers

In a large bowl, combine all ingredients except chocolate chips and cookies. Beat with an electric mixer on medium speed until well mixed. Cover and refrigerate for at least 30 minutes. Form into a ball and roll in chocolate chips. Wrap and refrigerate again until serving time. Serve cheese ball surrounded by cookies. Serves 12.

Fun for all ages! Animal crackers make whimsical dippers for sweet spreads. Set out a basketful, or give each guest her own little box.

Fuss-Free
Finger Foods

Mimi's Little Barbecue Sausages

Beverly Elkins
Bloomington, IN

These sausages are so easy and delicious...a great finger food for football games. My grandchildren call me "Mimi." The first time my youngest grandchild ate these little sausages, he asked me, "Are these Mimi's sausages?" I said, "Yes, they are!" and the name stuck. They are a favorite of all my family and they are requested at all our family get-togethers.

14-oz. pkg. mini smoked beef sausages
1 c. brown sugar, packed
1/2 c. catsup
1 T. Worcestershire sauce

Arrange sausages in a 13"x9" baking pan sprayed with non-stick vegetable spray; set aside. Combine remaining ingredients in a microwave-safe dish. Microwave on high for 2 minutes; stir, then microwave for one more minute. Spoon mixture over sausages. Bake, uncovered, at 350 degrees for 15 to 20 minutes. Serves 6 to 8.

Please the whole gang with an appetizer party! If your family & friends have different tastes, don't worry about deciding on the perfect main dish. Just serve 4 to 5 different appetizers and everyone can choose their favorites.

Fuss-Free Finger Foods

Pepperoni Pizza Pull

Kay Marone
Des Moines, IA

My family just loves monkey bread, so when I found this pizza-flavored version, I knew it would become a favorite!

1 c. shredded mozzarella cheese
1/4 c. grated Parmesan cheese
3-1/2 oz. pkg. sliced pepperoni, chopped
11-oz. tube refrigerated bread stick dough, cut into 1-inch pieces
Garnish: warmed pizza sauce

Combine cheeses and pepperoni in a bowl; set aside. Arrange 1/3 of dough pieces in a lightly greased 9"x5" loaf pan; top with 1/3 of cheese mixture. Repeat layering twice. Bake at 350 degrees for 25 minutes, or until golden. Cool in pan for 5 minutes; turn out of pan. Serve warm with pizza sauce. Serves 6 to 8.

Pizza Roll-Ups

Ildika Colley
Elkton, KY

My kids and I enjoyed making these tasty treats for an after-school snack. They'd be a hit at parties, too!

1/2 lb. ground beef
8-oz. can tomato sauce
1/2 c. shredded mozzarella cheese
1/2 t. dried oregano
2 8-oz. tubes refrigerated crescent rolls

Brown beef in a skillet over medium heat; drain. Remove from heat; stir in tomato sauce, cheese and oregano. Separate crescent rolls into 8 rectangles, pinching seams together. Along one long side of each rectangle, spoon 3 tablespoons beef mixture. Roll up rectangles jelly-roll style, starting on the same long side. Cut each roll into 3 pieces. Place rolls on a greased baking sheet, seam-side down, 2 inches apart. Bake at 375 degrees for 15 minutes, or until golden. Makes 2 dozen.

Spray plastic storage containers with non-stick vegetable spray before adding tomato-based sauces...no more stains!

Mexican Tortilla Roll-ups

Paula Summey
Dallas, GA

My daughter's second-grade school teacher gave me this tasty recipe many years ago. I have taken it to many potlucks and parties.

- 2 8-oz. pkgs. cream cheese, softened
- 2 4-oz. cans chopped green chiles, drained
- 2 3.8-oz. cans chopped black olives, drained
- 1 T. garlic powder
- 1 T. ground cumin
- 1 to 2 dashes hot pepper sauce
- salt and pepper to taste
- 10 flour tortillas
- Garnish: favorite salsa

In a large bowl, combine all ingredients except tortillas and salsa; stir until well mixed. Spread mixture lightly onto tortillas. Roll up and wrap tightly with plastic wrap. Refrigerate overnight. At serving time, unwrap roll-ups and slice. Serve with salsa. Makes about 2 dozen.

Try using colorful flavored wraps and tortillas when making roll-ups. Sun-dried tomato-basil, garlic-herb or cilantro really give them a zippy new look and taste.

Fuss-Free Finger Foods

Jalapeño Cheddar Balls

Cindy VonHentschel
Albuquerque, NM

I made up this recipe one year with some ingredients I had in the pantry and freezer. Now I make these for holiday potlucks and parties. People gobble them up, and I get a lot of really nice feedback.

16-oz. pk. ground pork breakfast sausage
2 to 3 large jalapeño peppers, finely diced and seeds removed
1/2 c. onion, finely diced
1 clove garlic, minced
1/2 c. shredded sharp Cheddar cheese
Optional: chilled jalapeño jelly

In a large bowl, combine all ingredients except optional jelly. Mix well. Using a small cookie scoop, form into one-inch meatballs. Place meatballs on a baking sheet sprayed with non-stick vegetable spray. Bake at 350 degrees for 10 to 15 minutes, until golden. Serve with jalapeño jelly, if desired. Makes 2 dozen.

Be a relaxed hostess. A day or two before your get-together, set out all the serving platters, baskets and dishes and label them... chicken wings, chips & dip and so on. When the big day arrives, you'll be able to set out all the goodies in seconds flat.

Bacon-Sausage Rye Crisps

Lisa Koehler
Oroville, CA

We sampled this appetizer at a party years ago and my husband said, "Get the recipe!" I've served it to my family & friends over the years and there is never any left at the end of the evening. Very easy and very yummy!

16-oz. pkg. bacon, crisply cooked and crumbled
16-oz. pkg. hot ground pork sausage, browned and drained
1-1/2 c. shredded Cheddar cheese
1/2 c. mayonnaise
1 loaf party rye bread

In a large bowl, combine cooked bacon and sausage, cheese and mayonnaise. Mix well. Spoon mixture onto rye bread slices and arrange on an ungreased baking sheet. Set oven to broil; set pan on top rack. Watching closely, broil until cheese melts and bread gets crisp around the edges. Serves 10.

Bake your bacon, no mess! Arrange slices on a broiler pan. Bake at 400 degrees for 12 to 15 minutes. Turn bacon over and bake for another 8 to 10 minutes, to desired crispness. Easy peasy!

Fuss-Free Finger Foods

Crispy Oven Wings

Claudia Keller
Carrollton, GA

My family loves these juicy wings so much, sometimes we have them for dinner. Serve with your favorite dipping sauce.

10 chicken wings, separated
1/3 c. all-purpose flour
1 T. paprika
1 t. garlic salt
1 t. pepper
1/4 to 1/2 t. cayenne pepper
3 T. butter, melted

Pat chicken wings dry with paper towels; set aside. In a plastic zipping bag, combine remaining ingredients except butter. Shake to mix; add wings to bag and shake until well coated. Spread melted butter on an aluminum foil-lined rimmed baking sheet. Arrange wings on pan; turn to coat. Bake at 425 degrees for 30 minutes. Turn wings over and bake for another 15 minutes, or until crisp, golden and juices run clear when pierced. Makes 20 pieces.

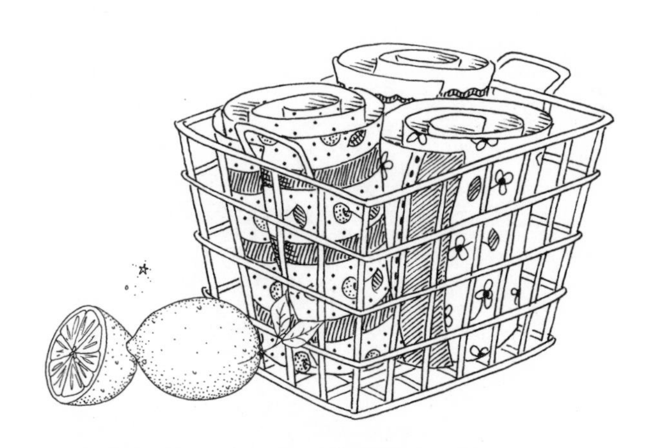

Alongside sticky finger foods like BBQ ribs and chicken wings, set out a basket of washcloths, dampened with lemon-scented water and warmed briefly in the microwave. Guests will thank you!

Front Porch Crackers

Marcia Shaffer
Conneaut Lake, PA

On hot sunny days, the kids love munching on these crackers alongside frosty glasses of lemonade.

1-3/4 c. mayonnaise, divided
3/4 c. shredded sharp Cheddar cheese
1/2 t. dry mustard
1/2 t. caraway seed
11-oz. pkg. buttery round crackers
1 c. onion, finely chopped

In a bowl, mix one cup mayonnaise, shredded cheese, mustard and caraway seed; set aside. Spread a thin layer of remaining mayonnaise on crackers; sprinkle with onion. Top each cracker with one teaspoon cheese mixture. Place crackers on ungreased baking sheets. Broil for several minutes, watching closely, until hot and cheese is melted. Serve immediately. Serves 10.

Guests are sure to appreciate pitchers of ice water they can help themselves to. Dress up ice cubes by dropping a fresh mint leaf or mini lemon twist into each compartment before adding water and freezing.

Fuss-Free Finger Foods

Bacon Crackers

Melissa Dattoli
Richmond, VA

This simple recipe may not sound like much, but the results are fantastic! I make these for parties and they're always loved by everyone. As the bacon cooks, some of the drippings soak into the crackers, making a crisp, flavorful base for the brown sugar-glazed bacon on top.

36 buttery club crackers
12 slices center-cut bacon, cut into thirds
3/4 to 1 c. light brown sugar, packed

Arrange crackers in a single layer on an aluminum foil-lined baking sheet. Top each cracker with a bacon piece, folding bacon if too wide for cracker. Sprinkle generously with brown sugar. Bake at 250 degrees for 30 to 45 minutes, until bacon is cooked. Let stand for 10 minutes before serving. Makes 3 dozen.

Ranch Pretzel Nibblers

Liz Blackstone
Racine, WI

If you need lots of crunchy snacks for munching, this recipe is terrific. Sometimes I use a mix of all three kinds of pretzels...friends like to pick out their favorite!

14-oz. pkg. sourdough pretzel nuggets
3 c. waffle-style pretzels or mini pretzel twists
1/3 c. oil
1-oz. pkg. ranch salad dressing mix

Spread all pretzels evenly on an ungreased 15"x10" jelly-roll pan; set aside. Combine oil and dressing mix in a small bowl; mix well and drizzle over pretzels. Stir to coat. Bake at 325 degrees for 10 minutes, stirring once. Spread pretzels on wax paper to cool. Store in an airtight container. Makes about 8 cups.

Heaven give you many, many merry days!

– William Shakespeare

Waffle Fry Nachos

Connie Hilty
Pearland, TX

Set the sheet pan right on the table...then just try to keep people away from these cheesy golden fries!

22-oz. pkg. frozen waffle fry potatoes
10 slices bacon, crisply cooked and crumbled
6-oz. can sliced black olives, drained
2 to 3 tomatoes, diced
3 green onions, sliced
2/3 c. favorite salsa
1-1/2 c. shredded Cheddar cheese
1-1/2 c. shredded Monterey Jack cheese
Garnish: sour cream

Arrange frozen potatoes in a single layer on a lightly greased 17"x11" jelly-roll pan. Bake at 450 degrees for 20 to 25 minutes, until crisp and lightly golden. Top with remaining ingredients except sour cream. Return to oven for another 5 minutes, or until cheeses are melted. Serve with sour cream. Serves 8.

Do-it-yourself nachos! Fill up the sections of a muffin tin with lots of tasty toppings, then let everyone mix & match their favorites. Fun for them...easy for you!

Golden Onion Rings

Doreen Knapp
Stanfordville, NY

Nothing tastes better than a great fried-up onion! Onion rings are one of my favorite little side dishes. Add any of your favorite seasonings to the onion rings while they are still warm, right out of the hot oil. Yum!

1 c. self-rising flour
1 c. cornmeal
1/2 t. salt
1/8 t. pepper
2 c. buttermilk or whole milk
2 egg whites, beaten
5 yellow sweet onions, sliced 1/4-inch thick
3 to 4 c. canola oil, divided
garlic powder, barbecue seasoning or Italian seasoning to taste

Separate onion slices into rings; set aside. In a shallow bowl, combine flour, cornmeal, salt and pepper. Beat in buttermilk or milk with a wooden spoon; beat in egg whites. Add onion rings to batter in bowl and turn until coated; set aside. Add 3 cups oil to a Dutch oven; heat to about 375 degrees over medium-high heat. Working in batches, add coated onion slices carefully to hot oil; cook until lightly golden on both sides. Add remaining oil, if needed. Drain on paper towels; sprinkle with desired seasoning while still warm. Makes 4 to 6 servings.

Warm and welcoming, any time of year! Light the path with luminarias... fill lunch bags about 1/3 full with sand, then nestle a votive in each. Light just in time to greet your first guests.

Spicy-Hot Sausages

Linda Rich
Bean Station, TN

My mother made this recipe often. It's so very simple and very good, if you have the patience to wait for the sausages to absorb the spices. We serve them with saltine crackers for a great snack or appetizer. For the tastiest results, be sure to use a really good brand of hot dogs.

4 lbs. hot dogs, cut into 1-inch to 2-inch pieces
2 large onions, sliced and separated into rings
4 c. white vinegar
3/4 c. sugar
4-1/2 oz. bottle hot pepper sauce
1/4 c. ground cumin
2 T. salt
2 to 4 t. pepper

Layer hot dogs and onions in a one-gallon canning jar (or 4 one-quart jars); set aside. Combine remaining ingredients in a saucepan over high heat. Bring to a boil; cook and stir for 3 minutes, or until sugar is dissolved. Pour vinegar mixture into jar, covering contents. Cover and refrigerate for 2 weeks before serving. The longer they set, the better they are! Makes 20 servings.

Set out a small discard dish for used toothpicks, to keep things tidy. Add one or 2 toothpicks in the dish so guests will get the idea!

Bread-and-Butter Refrigerator Pickles

Debbie Douma
Pensacola, FL

These are really tasty! Originally, I received a refrigerator pickle recipe from a friend 35 years ago, when she gave up trying to teach me how to can. I changed the white vinegar to cider vinegar and added celery seed to give them some zing. Will keep for weeks, but they never last that long around my house!

7 c. cucumbers, thinly sliced
2 T. salt
2 c. sugar
1 c. cider vinegar
1 t. celery seed

Place cucumber slices in a colander or bowl and sprinkle with salt. Let stand at least 2 hours; rinse and drain well. Meanwhile, combine sugar, vinegar and celery seed in a bowl. Let stand until sugar dissolves, stirring occasionally. Tightly pack cucumber slices in a quart-size canning jar; pour vinegar mixture into jar. Add lid and refrigerate for 24 hours before serving. Keep refrigerated up to one month.
Makes 18 servings.

Keep 'em cold! Fill a large galvanized tub with ice, then nestle bottles of soda in the ice. Tie a bottle opener to the handle with a ribbon...everyone can help themselves.

Dad's Special Meatballs

Gladys Kielar
Whitehouse, OH

Our party guests love Dad's meatballs! Serve in a small slow cooker set on low, with a jar of frilled toothpicks on the side.

1 lb. ground beef
1 egg, lightly beaten
1/2 c. soft bread crumbs
1/4 c. milk
1 t. salt
1/4 t. pepper
1/2 c. onion, minced
1 T. Worcestershire sauce
1/2 t. garlic salt
32-oz. jar grape jelly
12-oz. bottle chili sauce

In a large bowl, combine all ingredients except grape jelly and chili sauce. Mix well until blended. Form mixture into large balls, about 1-1/2 inches in diameter. Arrange on an ungreased rimmed baking sheet. Bake at 350 degrees for 15 minutes. Meanwhile, combine jelly and sauce in a large saucepan over medium heat. Cook and stir until blended and jelly is melted. Add meatballs to sauce; heat through over medium-low heat. Keep warm until ready to serve. Makes 2-1/2 dozen.

Vintage game boards make whimsical settings for game night buffets! Check the kids' closet for forgotten games or pick some up at yard sales. Cover with self-adhesive clear plastic for wipe-clean ease.

Teriyaki Chicken Wings

Marian Buckley
Fontana, CA

We love these old-school wings! Back in the 1980s, they were always on the buffet whenever my Aunt Sharon hosted a family gathering. Be sure to have plenty of napkins handy!

1 c. soy sauce
3/4 c. sugar
1/2 c. brown sugar, packed
1/4 c. pineapple juice
1/4 c. water
2 T. oil
1 t. garlic powder
1 t. ground ginger
4 lbs. chicken wings, separated

In a very large bowl, combine all ingredients except chicken wings; stir until sugars dissolve. Add wings; toss gently to coat. Cover and refrigerate at least 2 hours to marinate. Transfer wings to a 6-quart slow cooker. Add one cup of the marinade to slow cooker; discard remaining marinade. Cover and cook on high setting for 3-1/2 to 4-1/2 hours, until chicken juices run clear when pierced. If desired, transfer wings to a broiler pan; broil for 2 to 3 minutes, until golden. Makes about 4 dozen.

For the little ones, cover a table with a sheet of butcher paper. Place a flowerpot filled with markers, crayons and stickers in the middle...they'll have a blast decorating the table!

Merry Nutcracker Munch

Amy Thomason Hunt
Traphill, NC

Yummy for snacking while trimming the Christmas tree... or any other occasion year 'round!

12 c. popped popcorn
1 lb. bacon, crisply cooked and crumbled
12-oz. can mixed nuts, toasted
1/2 c. sunflower seeds, toasted
1/4 c. butter, melted and divided
3 T. grated Parmesan cheese, divided

Place popcorn in a large bowl; remove any unpopped kernels. Add crumbled bacon, mixed nuts and sunflower seeds. Drizzle with half of the melted butter; sprinkle with half the Parmesan cheese and toss to coat. Repeat with remaining butter and cheese; serve warm. Makes 12 servings.

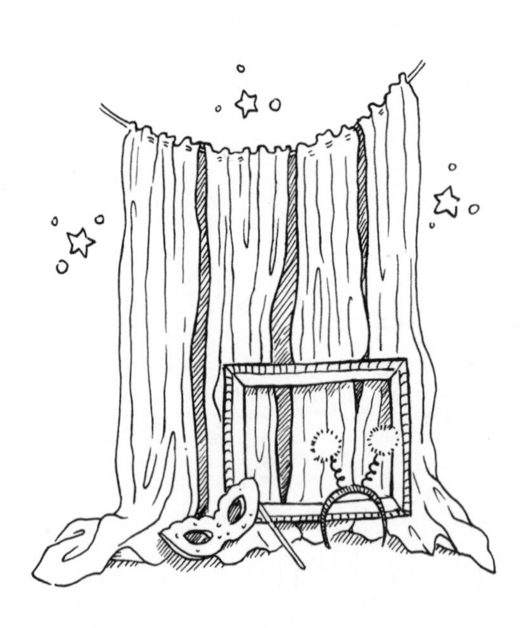

A photo booth is fun for guests of all ages...instant mementos too. Choose plain drapes as a backdrop, or hang up a colorful plastic tablecloth. Add a large picture frame and some props, then let everyone take their best shot!

Fuss-Free Finger Foods

Toasted Chili Nuts

Shirley Howie
Foxboro, MA

I like to serve these yummy toasted nuts as part of my Christmas Eve buffet. They're always a hit!

2 T. butter
2 T. Worcestershire sauce
1 t. chili powder
1/4 t. cayenne pepper
1/4 t. onion salt
2 c. walnut or pecan halves

In a saucepan over low heat, combine butter, Worcestershire sauce and seasonings. Cook and stir until butter melts. Spread nuts in an ungreased 9"x9" baking pan. Toss with butter mixture. Bake at 350 degrees for 12 to 15 minutes, stirring occasionally, until toasted. Spread nuts on aluminum foil; cool. Store in an airtight container. Makes 2 cups.

Spicy Ranch Party Pretzels

Janie Branstetter
Duncan, OK

A one-of-a-kind snack mix you just can't get enough of. You may have to double this recipe!

3/4 c. oil
1-oz. pkg. ranch salad dressing mix
1 T. garlic salt
1 T. lemon pepper
1 T. cayenne pepper
16-oz. pkg. mini pretzel twists or thins

Combine all ingredients except pretzels in a large plastic zipping bag; mix well. Add pretzels to bag; shake to coat well. Spread pretzels on an ungreased baking sheet; let stand until dry. Store in an airtight container. Serves 10 to 12.

Spoon popcorn or snack mix into a punch bowl and add a scoop. A stack of snack-size paper bags nearby will make it easy for everyone to help themselves.

Deluxe Jalapeño Poppers

JoAnn Kurtz
Wichita Falls, TX

When I made these for a Christmas party at church, they were the first appetizer that disappeared! Now I make them year 'round. I always get asked for the recipe and I'm happy to share it. You can choose to make them as mild or as spicy as you like.

- 12 to 15 jalapeño peppers, halved lengthwise
- 8 thick-cut slices bacon
- 16-oz. pkg. mild or spicy ground pork breakfast sausage
- 1/2 c. sweet onion, finely chopped
- 8-oz. pkg. cream cheese, cubed and softened
- 1 c. shredded Cheddar or Pepper Jack cheese
- Garnish: ranch salad dressing

Scoop out all or some of the seeds from jalapeño halves, depending spiciness desired; set aside. Cook bacon in a skillet over medium heat until crisp; set aside to drain on paper towels. Meanwhile, brown sausage with onion in another skillet over medium heat; drain and stir in cheeses. With a teaspoon, generously stuff sausage mixture into pepper halves; sprinkle with crumbled bacon. At this point, pepper halves may be wrapped in plastic wrap and frozen up to 2 weeks. To serve, arrange on baking sheets. Bake on top rack of oven at 425 degrees for 30 minutes, or until bubbly and golden. Serve warm, with ranch dressing for dipping. Makes 2 to 2-1/2 dozen.

When preparing hot peppers, be sure to wear plastic gloves while chopping and slicing. Don't touch your face, lips or eyes while you're working! Just toss away the gloves when you're done.

Fuss-Free Finger Foods

Spicy Chorizo-Stuffed Mushrooms

Courtney Stultz
Weir, KS

These are so simple to make, yet full of delicious flavor. Stuffed mushrooms are one of my husband's favorite appetizers, but I get bored with the same flavors. He also loves spicy food, so I decided to make these spicy mushrooms. Great for holidays, game days, tailgates or even just for dinner!

2 lbs. small portabella mushroom caps
16-oz. pkg. spicy ground pork chorizo sausage
1 c. shredded Cheddar cheese, divided
1/4 c. green onions, diced
2 T. fresh cilantro, finely chopped
Optional: ranch salad dressing or chipotle mayonnaise

Arrange mushroom caps in a single layer in a lightly greased 13"x9" baking pan; set aside. In a large skillet, cook sausage over medium heat until no longer pink; drain. Stir in 3/4 cup cheese and onions, mixing well. Spoon sausage mixture into mushrooms; top with remaining cheese. Arrange in an ungreased 13"x9" baking pan. Bake at 400 degrees for about 20 minutes, until mushrooms are soft. Remove from oven; top with cilantro. Serve with salad dressing or mayonnaise, if desired. Serves 10.

Serve easy-to-handle foods and beverages at tables in several different rooms around the house. Guests will be able to snack and mingle easily.

Shrimp Antipasto

Sharon Tillman
Hampton, VA

Put together this delicious appetizer with just a stop at the deli counter and a few pantry items. Pull it from the fridge at serving time...your guests will be so impressed!

1-1/2 lbs. medium cooked shrimp, shells removed
1/2 lb. provolone cheese, cut into 1/2-inch cubes
6-oz. can black olives, drained
1 c. olive oil
2/3 c. lemon juice
2 T. sugar
2 T. Dijon mustard
1-1/2 t. dried thyme
1 t. salt
1/4 lb. Genoa salami, cut into 1/2-inch cubes
1 red pepper, cut into 1-inch squares

Combine shrimp, cheese cubes and olives in a large shallow dish; set aside. In a small bowl, combine remaining ingredients except salami and red pepper; pour over shrimp mixture. Cover and refrigerate for 6 hours, stirring occasionally. At serving time, mix in salami and red pepper; toss well. Transfer mixture to a serving bowl, discarding dressing. Serve with frilled toothpicks. Makes 8 cups.

Check out the neighborhood dollar store, where all kinds of colorful, clever items for table decorating, serving and party favors can be found. Big fun at a small price!

Festive Shrimp Pinwheels

Becky Butler
Keller, TX

These are easy to make and irresistible on a buffet table. To cut the rolls of dough into slices, I like to use a length of plain dental floss. Just slip it under the roll, cross it over the top and pull...nice, clean cuts every time!

8-oz. tube refrigerated crescent dinner rolls
1/3 c. garlic & herb spreadable cream cheese
1/2 c. cooked shrimp, coarsely chopped
1/2 t. Cajun or Creole seasoning blend
2 T. green onions, chopped

Unroll dough and separate into 2 long rectangles. Press each into a 12-inch by 4-inch rectangle; firmly press perforations to seal. Spread cheese over each rectangle. Sprinkle each with shrimp, seasoning and onions; press in lightly. Starting on one short side, roll up each rectangle; press edge to seal. Cut each roll into 8 slices. Arrange slices cut-side down on a lightly greased baking sheet. Bake at 350 degrees for 15 to 20 minutes, until edges are golden. Immediately remove from baking sheet; serve warm. Makes 16 pieces.

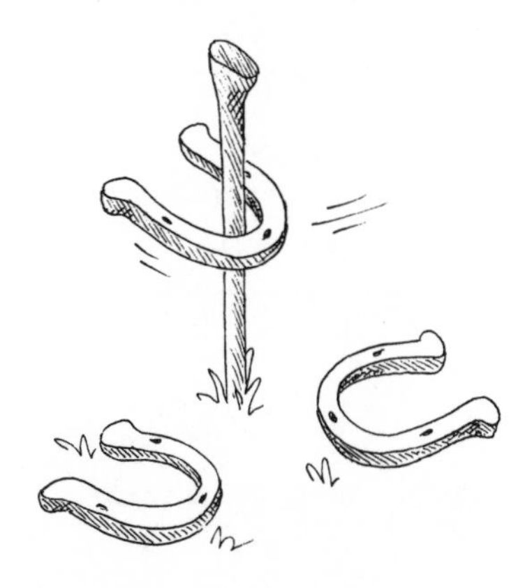

Host a family reunion this year! Plan a full day of activities... horseshoe toss, softball and lots of catching up! Load up picnic tables with simple, down-home favorites, share recipes and memories and take lots of pictures.

Crunchy Sweet Snack Mix

Emily Martin
Ontario, Canada

A great make-ahead mix! I like to set out bowls of this delectable treat for everyone to munch on while I'm putting the finishing touches on dinner.

2 egg whites
2 T. soy sauce
1 T. water
3 6-oz. pkgs. whole almonds
6-oz. pkg. sweetened dried cranberries
5-oz. container chow mein noodles
1/2 c. sugar
1 t. cinnamon
1/2 t. salt

In a large bowl, whisk egg whites for 30 seconds, until lightly frothy. Add soy sauce and water; whisk for an additional 30 seconds. Add almonds, cranberries and noodles; stir until well coated and set aside. Combine sugar, cinnamon and salt in a small bowl. Blend well and sprinkle over almond mixture; toss to coat. Spread mixture evenly on a lightly greased 15"x10" jelly-roll pan. Bake at 250 degrees for one hour, stirring every 15 minutes. Cool completely. Store in an airtight container. Makes about 8 cups.

Pick up some plastic icing cones when you shop for baking supplies. Filled with snack mix, tied with curling ribbon and placed in a wire cupcake stand, they make fun gifts to keep on hand for drop-in guests.

Sweet & Spicy Roasted Pecans

Lisa Ann Panzino DiNunzio
Vineland, NJ

Want a simply delicious and easy snack to set out for visitors during the holidays? This is it!

2 egg whites
1/2 c. sugar
1 t. vanilla extract
1 T. cinnamon
1/2 t. salt
Optional: 1/8 t. cayenne pepper
1 lb. pecan halves

In a large bowl, beat egg whites until frothy, but not stiff. Stir in sugar, vanilla and seasonings. Add pecans; stir until well coated. Spread nuts evenly onto a parchment paper-lined baking sheet. Bake at 225 degrees for 50 to 60 minutes, stirring every 15 minutes. Cool completely. Store in an airtight container. Makes about 4 cups.

Welcome guests with a year 'round wreath! Start with a grapevine wreath, then add greenery and a homespun bow. Decorations can be changed for each season...mini flags and sparkly stars for summer, mini pumpkins for fall, and so on. Store everything in a box kept handy for greeting the next season.

Red Beet Deviled Eggs

Georgia Muth
Penn Valley, CA

I prepare these deviled eggs for holidays and parties. They're a favorite appetizer at our table. For a shortcut, I have left the yolks intact and skipped the deviling step. Just leave the yolks intact, slice in half and you have a tasty hard-boiled red egg.

1 doz. eggs, hard-boiled
2 15-oz. cans sliced beets, drained and 1 c. juice reserved
1 c. brown sugar, packed
3/4 c. cider vinegar
1/4 c. water
3/8 t. pickling spice
1/2 t. salt
3 T. mayonnaise
2 T. celery, finely diced
salt and pepper to taste

Peel eggs and set aside in a large bowl. In a large saucepan, combine reserved beet juice, brown sugar, vinegar, water, pickling spice and salt. Bring to a boil over medium-high heat. Reduce heat to medium-low and simmer for 15 minutes. Add sliced beets to mixture; spoon beets and liquid over eggs. Cover and refrigerate overnight. Drain, discarding liquid; set aside sliced beets. Drain eggs on paper towels and pat dry. Cut eggs in half and remove yolks to a bowl. Mash yolks with a fork; mix with mayonnaise, celery, salt and pepper. Spoon yolk mixture into egg whites. Serve sliced beets alongside eggs. Makes 2 dozen.

Deviled eggs are sure to be a hit at just about any kind of gathering. If you don't have a special egg plate, nestle the eggs in a bed of shredded lettuce or curly parsley to keep them from sliding around...they'll look scrumptious!

Fuss-Free Finger Foods

Parmesan Broccoli Balls

Linda Diepholz
Lakeville, MN

This is an appetizer that I have been making for years. I serve it every year with my Thanksgiving and Christmas Eve dinners. These are also delicious to snack on...I even like them cold!

10-oz. pkg. frozen chopped broccoli, thawed
6-oz. pkg. chicken-flavored stuffing mix
1/2 c. shredded Parmesan cheese
3/4 c. onion, chopped
6 eggs, beaten
3/4 c. butter, melted
1/2 t. garlic salt
1 t. pepper

Place broccoli in a saucepan; cover with water. Add lid; bring to a boil over medium heat. Cook for 5 minutes. Uncover; continue cooking for 2 to 3 minutes, until tender. Remove from heat; drain and cool. Transfer broccoli to a large bowl; add remaining ingredients and mix well. Cover and refrigerate for one hour to overnight, until moisture has been absorbed. Form the chilled mixture into one-inch balls; arrange on a lightly greased baking sheet. Bake at 325 degrees for 15 to 20 minutes, until golden. Makes 2 dozen.

For a quick snack that everybody loves, nothing beats a big bowl of popcorn...perfect if dinner will be delayed, too! Jazz it up with a sprinkle of grated Parmesan cheese or taco seasoning, or serve it the classic way, with butter and salt.

Hot Antipasto Squares

Theresa Jakab
Milford, CT

A friend shared this recipe with me years ago. There are several versions out there...this version is mine! It's great warm, and also good cold.

3 eggs
1/4 c. grated Parmesan cheese
2 12-oz. tubes refrigerated buttery crescent rolls
1/4 lb. sliced deli baked ham
1/4 lb. sliced deli American cheese
1/4 lb. sliced deli Genoa salami
1/4 lb. sliced deli Swiss cheese
1/4 lb. sliced pepperoni
12-oz. jar roasted red peppers, well drained
garlic powder, salt and pepper to taste
1/4 lb. sliced deli provolone cheese

Beat eggs in a small bowl; stir in Parmesan cheese and set aside. Unroll one tube of crescent rolls; layer in the bottom of a lightly greased 13"x9" baking pan. Layer ingredients as follows: ham, American cheese, salami, Swiss cheese, pepperoni and red peppers. Sprinkle with seasonings; brush with 2/3 of egg mixture and layer with provolone cheese. Layer remaining tube of rolls on top; brush with remaining egg mixture. Cover with aluminum foil. Bake at 350 degrees for 45 minutes. Remove foil and bake for 10 to 15 minutes more, until golden. Cool for about 15 minutes; cut into squares. Makes 2 dozen.

Friendship is born at that moment when one person says to another, What! You, too? I thought I was the only one.

– C. S. Lewis

Sweet-and-Sour Sauce Meatballs

Rebecca Meadows
Hinton, WV

This sauce recipe has become a favorite! It came from a friendly worker doing a sampling for frozen meatballs at my local bulk food store. While taste testing, I told the lady how much I loved the sweet-and-sour meatballs and wished I had the recipe for the sauce. She kindly gave me her worn copy of the recipe, because she knew it by heart. Since then, the recipe has been passed along to many others that I've come in contact with. It's great for parties, church picnics, showers and even tailgating parties.

48-oz. pkg. frozen Italian meatballs
20-oz. can pineapple chunks
1 c. sugar
1 c. white vinegar
1 c. catsup
1 c. water

Place meatballs in a 5-quart slow cooker; set aside. Combine pineapple with juice and remaining ingredients in a saucepan over medium heat. Bring to a low boil; cook and stir until sugar dissolves. Simmer for 5 minutes; spoon over meatballs. Cover and cook on low setting for 4 hours, or until meatballs are heated through. Makes 4 to 5 dozen.

Safety first! Keep hot foods hot, cold foods cold, and don't leave anything at room temperature longer than 2 hours, even if the food still looks just fine.

Chutney Chicken Bites

Elizabeth Smithson
Mayfield, KY

This is a standby, an old, old recipe I found in a farm magazine. I use canned chicken and it works fine. Everyone wants me to make it for any occasion. I fixed it for the holiday cookie exchange this year.

1/2 c. cream cheese, softened
2 T. mayonnaise
1 c. cooked chicken, chopped
1 c. almonds, finely chopped
1 T. fruit chutney, chopped
1 t. curry powder
1/2 t. salt
1/2 c. flaked coconut

In a bowl, blend together cream cheese and mayonnaise. Add chicken, almonds, chutney and seasonings; mix well. Shape into marble-size balls and roll in coconut. Cover and chill until serving time. Serves 12 to 15.

Crunchy Artichoke Fries

Jill Burton
Gooseberry Patch

A warm veggie treat that everyone loves! Serve with lemon wedges for squeezing over the artichokes.

1/2 c. all-purpose flour
2 eggs, beaten
1 c. panko bread crumbs
salt and pepper to taste
12-oz. jar marinated quartered artichoke hearts, drained
1 to 2 T. olive oil

Place flour in a shallow bowl, eggs in a second bowl and panko crumbs in a third; season each bowl with salt and pepper. Pat artichokes dry with paper towels. Coat artichokes in flour; dip into eggs and roll in bread crumbs. Arrange on an ungreased baking sheet; drizzle with olive oil. Bake at 400 degrees for 25 minutes, or until crisp and golden. Serve warm. Serves 4.

Bright-colored plastic Frisbees make great no-spill holders for flimsy paper plates. Afterwards, kids can take them home as an extra party favor.

Fuss-Free Finger Foods

Mock Pizzas

Nancy Jones
Tempe, AZ

My mother Helen used to make these during the holidays. Everyone in our family of eight children gobbled them up! Made several days ahead of time, these are stored in the freezer, and can be baked whenever unexpected guests come by, or just because you are craving them.

1lb. ground pork sausage
1 lb. ground beef
16-oz. pkg. pasteurized process cheese, cubed
1 t. dried oregano
1 t. garlic powder
2 loaves party rye bread

Brown and crumble beef in a large skillet over medium heat; drain and set aside. Brown sausage in same skillet; drain and set aside. Reduce heat to medium-low. Add cheese to skillet; cook and stir until melted. Add seasonings and mix very well. Return meats to skillet. Cook, stirring constantly, until well mixed with the cheese. Drop teaspoonfuls of mixture onto slices of bread; place on wax paper-lined baking sheets. Top with another piece of wax paper; continue layering. Place baking sheets in the freezer until partly frozen. Transfer to a plastic freezer bag to store. To serve, place desired amount of mini pizzas on wax paper-lined baking sheets. Bake at 350 degrees for 15 to 25 minutes, until bubbly and golden. Serves 10.

Alongside the disposable cups, set a jar filled with marker pens. Guests can write their names on the cups, for less waste.

Buffalo Chicken Skewers

Audrey Lett
Newark, DE

A yummy variation on boneless wings! I was happy to find this recipe...I have friends who love buffalo wings, but are a little "iffy" about chicken bones. Everyone loves these!

8 wooden skewers
1 to 2 T. olive oil
1 lb. boneless, skinless chicken tenderloins, halved lengthwise
1 t. garlic powder
1 t. salt
1 t. pepper
1 c. buffalo wing sauce
Garnish: blue cheese salad dressing, celery sticks

Soak skewers in water for 30 minutes. Line a rimmed baking sheet with aluminum foil; drizzle with olive oil and set aside. Thread each chicken tenderloin onto a wooden skewer; arrange on baking sheet. Combine seasonings and sprinkle over chicken. Bake at 425 degrees for 10 minutes; remove from oven. Drizzle chicken with wing sauce, coating well. Return to oven and bake another 5 minutes longer, or until cooked through. Serve skewers with salad dressing and celery sticks. Makes 8 skewers.

Whip up some fresh blue cheese dressing to serve with chicken wings and salads. Whisk together one cup buttermilk, 1/2 cup sour cream and 1/4 cup mayonnaise; stir in 3/4 cup crumbled blue cheese. Add salt and pepper to taste...scrumptious!

Chicken Macho Nachos

Jill Ball
Highland, UT

This is a must for any friendly get-together...but watch out, people will gather around it! It's so easy to make in your slow cooker.

5 boneless, skinless chicken breasts
15-1/2 oz. can black beans, drained
15-1/4 oz. can corn, drained
16-oz. jar favorite salsa
8-oz. pkg. cream cheese, cubed and softened
corn or tortilla chips

Place chicken in a 5-quart slow cooker; top with beans, corn and salsa. Cover and cook on low setting for 4 to 5 hours, until chicken is very tender. Shred chicken and return to slow cooker; stir in cream cheese. Cover and let stand for 30 minutes, or until cream cheese is melted. Stir well. Serve chicken mixture with corn or tortilla chips. Serves 12.

A make-it-yourself pizza party is great for pizza-loving youngsters! It's cheaper than ordering from a pizza shop and doubles as a fun activity. Set out ready-to-bake pizza crusts and lots of toppings...let guests be creative!

Pat's Cheesy Appetizer Bread

Pat Martin
Riverside, CA

Ten years ago, I found this recipe online and adapted it to my family's taste. I have been making it for our Christmas dinner ever since. Everyone loves it and it can be further adapted with your favorite cheeses. Stack up the rolls in a basket to serve, cut into appetizer-size portions.

16-oz. pkg. shredded Italian-blend cheese
6-oz. pkg. shredded low-fat Swiss cheese
1 c. mayonnaise
1/2 c. chopped green or black olives, drained
1-1/2 t. garlic powder
6 soft sub rolls, halved lengthwise

In a large bowl, combine all ingredients except rolls. Mix well; spread onto cut sides of rolls. Arrange rolls on a broiler pan. Broil, 6 inches from heat, for one minute, or until golden and cheese is melted. Slice into portions as desired; serve warm. Rolls with topping may be assembled ahead and kept refrigerated; let stand at room temperature for 15 to 30 minutes before broiling. Makes 12 to 24 servings.

Make it easy for your guests to find the way to your home. Simply tie a bouquet of balloons to your mailbox or front porch.

Fuss-Free Finger Foods

Easy Bruschetta

Charlotte Smith
Alexandria, PA

This is a great appetizer...very tasty and pretty easy. A wonderful way to enjoy ripe summer tomatoes!

1 lb. ripe tomatoes, diced
1 red Spanish onion, finely diced
2 T. olive oil
salt and pepper to taste
1 loaf Italian bread, thinly sliced on the diagonal
2 to 3 cloves garlic, halved
Garnish: shredded fresh basil

In a bowl, combine tomatoes, onion and olive oil. Season with salt and pepper; set aside. Lightly toast bread slices. While still warm, rub both sides of bread with cut side of garlic. Spoon tomato mixture over bread. Serve warm, topped with basil. Serves 6 to 8.

Dessa's "Too Bad" Bread

Jennifer Hatridge
Lancaster, PA

As a child, I remember my Aunt Dessa introducing our family to this simple yet tasty bread with an odd name. "It's too bad there isn't more of that bread left!" was always the cry for seconds and thirds.

1 loaf Italian or French bread, halved lengthwise
1/2 c. butter, softened
garlic salt to taste
2 c. shredded Cheddar cheese
4 green onions, chopped

Spread cut sides of loaf evenly with butter. Sprinkle with garlic salt, cheese and onions. Place cut-side up on an aluminum foil-lined baking sheet. Bake at 350 degrees for 10 to 12 minutes, until cheese is melted. Slice and serve warm. Makes 12 servings.

Besides bread, a serrated bread knife is great for easily cutting juicy ripe tomatoes...no squishing!

Crabbies

Ildika Colley
Elkton, KY

These are one of our favorite appetizers for watching the big football game on television with family & friends. For easy prep, the crabmeat spread can be made ahead of time and tucked in the fridge, then later top the muffins, bake and serve hot.

5-oz. jar sharp Cheddar cheese spread
1/4 c. butter, softened
1 T. onion, minced
1 t. garlic, minced
7-oz. can crabmeat, well drained and flaked
12-oz. pkg. English muffins, split
paprika to taste

In a bowl, combine cheese spread, butter, onion and garlic; blend in crabmeat. Spread crab mixture on cut sides of muffin halves; sprinkle with paprika. Arrange on an ungreased baking sheet. Bake at 350 degrees for 12 to 15 minutes, until bubbly and golden. Cut each muffin half into 4 to 6 wedges; serve warm. Serves 20.

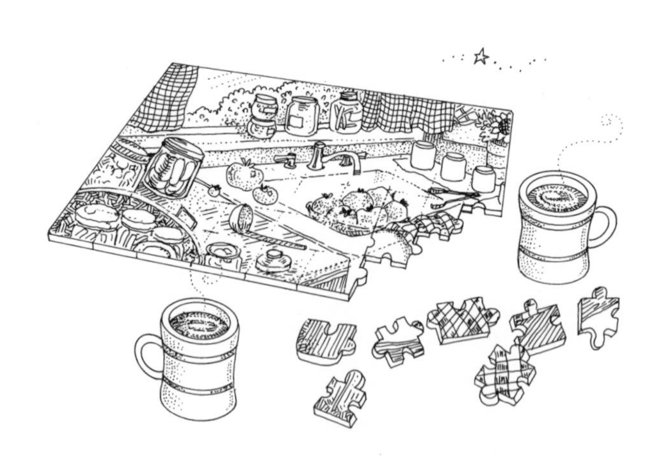

Set out a jigsaw puzzle on a table in a quiet corner. Guests are sure to enjoy fitting a few pieces into place as they relax with a plateful of appetizers.

Fuss-Free Finger Foods

Olive Cheese Balls

Elaine Divis
Sioux City, IA

My mother made these for every get-together back in the 60s and 70s. You can use either black olives or green pimento-stuffed olives... the black olives are our favorite.

8-oz. pkg. finely shredded sharp Cheddar cheese
1-1/4 c. all-purpose flour
1/2 c. butter, melted
48 black or green stuffed olives, drained and patted dry

In a bowl, stir together cheese, flour and butter until well blended. Shape dough around olives by teaspoonfuls; form into balls. Place on an ungreased baking sheet. Cover and refrigerate at least one hour, up to 24 hours. Bake at 400 degrees for 15 to 20 minutes, until lightly golden. Serve warm or cold. Makes 4 dozen.

Blue Cheese Pillows

Becky Myers
Ashland, OH

These little appetizers have been a family tradition on Christmas for years. Even if you don't like blue cheese, you will love them... they're quick & easy and yummy!

8-oz. tube refrigerated Pillsbury biscuits, quartered
1/2 c. butter, melted
4-oz. container crumbled blue cheese

Arrange biscuit quarters on a lightly greased 15"x10" jelly-roll pan; set aside. In a bowl, stir together melted butter and cheese. Spoon over biscuits, coating well. Bake at 350 degrees for about 8 minutes, until golden. Serve warm. Serves 10 to 12.

A 250-degree oven keeps hot appetizers toasty until you're ready to serve them.

Arkansas Firecrackers

Pam Massey
Marshall, AR

These crunchy, savory crackers make a wonderful addition to gift baskets. Add more red pepper flakes if you like your firecrackers extra spicy! Sometimes I change it up by adding some pretzels.

2 c. canola oil
2 1-oz. pkgs. ranch seasoning mix
1 T. red pepper flakes
1 t. onion powder
1 t. garlic powder
11-oz. pkg. mini saltine crackers
2 to 3 sleeves round wheat crackers

In a large bowl, combine all ingredients except crackers; stir well. Add all crackers and mix until well coated. Let stand overnight at room temperature, stirring occasionally. Spread crackers evenly on an ungreased 15"x10" jelly-roll pan. Bake at 200 degrees for one hour, stirring every 15 minutes. Cool completely. Store in airtight containers. Serves 12.

For an easy yet elegant appetizer, try a cheese platter. Choose a soft cheese, a hard cheese and a semi-soft or crumbly cheese. Add a basket of crisp crackers, crusty baguette slices and some sliced apples or pears. So simple, yet sure to please guests.

Sandwiches *for Any Occasion*

Mom's BBQ Sandwiches

Rhonda Millerman
Cameron, WI

This was my mom's favorite to make for family birthday parties. Growing up with six siblings, we were blessed with Mom's home-cooked meals. These were a fave of mine! She passed away several years ago, and I'm happy to share a part of her when I make these for my family.

1-1/2 lbs. ground beef
1/2 c. onion, chopped
10-3/4 oz. can tomato soup
1/2 c. catsup
1/3 c. vinegar
1/4 c. brown sugar, packed
1 t. mustard
salt and pepper to taste
10 to 12 hamburger buns, split and buttered

In a large skillet over medium heat, brown beef with onion until no longer pink. Drain and rinse beef; return to skillet. Stir in remaining ingredients except buns. Heat through over medium-low heat until bubbly, stirring often. Serve on buttered buns. Makes 10 to 12 sandwiches.

Mailing out invitations? Check at the post office for fun stamps that go with the occasion's theme. You'll find stamps that depict sports, cartoons, pets, nature...even stamps that proclaim "Celebrate!"

Sandwiches *for Any Occasion*

Barbecue Pork Sandwiches

Charity Thomas
Fort Worth, TX

This recipe came from a dear friend who taught second grade with me. She fixed it for a social after school one day. Everyone loved it, because it was a quick fix for busy moms like ourselves. Her secret was slow-cooking the pork and using Kansas City-style sauce.

3-1/2 lb. Boston butt pork roast
salt and pepper to taste
2 18-oz. bottles Kansas City-Style barbecue sauce
10 sandwich buns, split

Season roast with salt and pepper; place in a 5-quart slow cooker. Add enough water to partially cover roast. Cover and cook on low setting for 8 to 10 hours, until fork-tender. Remove roast to a plate and cool; drain slow cooker and wipe clean. Shred roast with a large fork and knife; return to slow cooker. Stir in barbecue sauce. Cover and cook on low setting for at least 2 hours. Serve pork in sandwich buns. Makes 10 sandwiches.

Zesty Chicken Sandwiches

Toni Groves
Benld, IL

My niece makes this slow-cooker recipe for family gatherings on Christmas Eve. It never lasts long! Serve on your choice of rolls.

3 lbs. boneless, skinless chicken breasts
12-oz. jar zesty banana pepper rings
2 cubes chicken bouillon
1-1/2 c. water
10 to 12 sandwich rolls, split

Place chicken in a 4-quart slow cooker. Top with undrained pepper rings, bouillon cubes and water. Cover and cook on low setting for 8 to 10 hours, until chicken is very tender. Remove chicken; shred with a fork and return to slow cooker. Stir; cover and cook for another one to 2 hours. Serve on rolls. Makes 10 to 12 sandwiches.

Paper coffee filters make tidy toss-away holders for sandwiches, hot dog buns and tacos.

Easy Roast Beef Sliders

Tori Willis
Champaign, IL

I love to bake up a panful of these yummy sandwiches. They're great for parties and quick meals...hungry kids love 'em. For a flavor change, swap out the horseradish for Dijon mustard.

12-oz. pkg. Hawaiian sweet rolls
1/4 c. creamy horseradish
1 lb. thinly sliced deli roast beef
6 slices provolone or mozzarella cheese
1/3 c. butter, melted
2 T. Worcestershire sauce
1 T. dried parsley
2 t. brown sugar, packed
1/4 t. onion powder

Cut the whole package of rolls in half horizontally. Place the bottom half in a lightly greased 13"x9" baking pan. Spread cut side of rolls with horseradish; arrange roast beef and cheese slices over rolls. Add top half of rolls; set aside. In a small bowl, combine remaining ingredients; spoon evenly over sandwiches. Cover and refrigerate for one hour to overnight. Bake, uncovered, at 350 degrees for 15 to 20 minutes, until cheese is melted and rolls are golden. Cut apart sandwiches; serve warm. Makes 12 sandwiches.

Be a relaxed hostess...choose foods that can be prepared in advance. At serving time, simply pull dishes from the fridge, or pop into a hot oven as needed. A make-ahead sandwich like Easy Beef Rolls is perfect.

Sandwiches for Any Occasion

Italian Beef Sandwiches

Tiffney Batton
Morgantown, WV

We love college football and tailgating in the fall. Our tailgate has become known for my Italian beef sandwiches... people line up at the grill, just waiting for a bite!

2 to 3-lb. beef chuck roast
12-oz. jar mild or hot yellow pepper rings, drained and liquid reserved
10-1/2 oz. can beef broth, divided
1-oz. pkg. zesty Italian salad dressing mix
1 small yellow onion, sliced and separated into rings
10 French baguette rolls, split and toasted
Optional: mozzarella cheese slices

Place roast in a 4-quart slow cooker. Top with pepper rings, half of reserved pepper liquid, half of beef broth, salad dressing mix and onion rings. Cover and cook on low setting for 10 to 12 hours, until roast is very tender. Remove roast from slow cooker. Shred with 2 forks and return to slow cooker. Add some of remaining pepper liquid and beef broth, if needed; heat through. Serve beef on toasted baguette rolls. If desired, top with mozzarella cheese and place under broiler to crisp. Makes 10 sandwiches.

Turn your favorite shredded pork and beef into party food... meatballs too. Serve up bite-size portions on slider buns. Guests will love sampling a little of everything.

Artichoke Tuna Melt

Sandra Sullivan
Aurora, CO

This is no ordinary tuna sandwich! It's topped with tasty, healthy ingredients, perfect for sharing at get-togethers. It's my favorite sandwich...I predict it will become yours too.

1 loaf French bread, halved
1 T. olive oil
1 clove garlic, halved
3/4 c. mayonnaise
1 T. lemon juice
1 T. Dijon mustard
1/2 t. garlic powder
1/2 t. pepper
2 10-oz. cans white tuna packed in water, drained and flaked
14-oz. can artichoke hearts, drained, rinsed and chopped
1 c. fresh baby spinach
2 plum tomatoes, sliced
1 c. shredded mozzarella cheese

Place halves of loaf cut-side up on an ungreased baking sheet; brush with olive oil. Broil 4 to 6 inches from heat for 2 to 3 minutes, until golden. Rub cut sides of garlic clove over warm bread; discard garlic. In a large bowl, combine mayonnaise, lemon juice, mustard and seasonings; stir in tuna and artichokes. Arrange spinach over bread; top with tuna mixture, tomatoes and cheese. Broil for one minute longer, or until cheese is melted. Slice and serve. Makes 6 servings.

The best kind of friend is the kind you can sit on a porch swing with, never say a word, then walk away feeling like it was the best conversation you've ever had.

– Arnold Glasow

Sandwiches for Any Occasion

Grilled Veggie Sammies

Amy Thomason Hunt
Traphill, NC

Oh-so good and cheesy! Delicious just the way it is, or add some thin-sliced cooked chicken for a hearty sandwich.

1 small zucchini, cut into 4 thin slices lengthwise
2 portabella mushroom caps, cut in half
2 T. olive oil
salt and pepper to taste
1 loaf French bread, halved lengthwise
1 large tomato, cut into 4 slices
4 slices smoked provolone cheese
8 fresh basil or spinach leaves

Brush zucchini and mushrooms with olive oil; sprinkle with salt and pepper. Place on a preheated grill and close lid. Grill for 5 to 7 minutes, turning once, until tender. Spread cut sides of bread with Lemon-Garlic Mayonnaise. On bottom half of loaf, layer zucchini, mushrooms, tomato, cheese and basil or spinach leaves. Add top of loaf; cut into 4 pieces. Makes 4 sandwiches.

Lemon-Garlic Mayonnaise:

1/4 c. mayonnaise
1 T. lemon juice
1 t. garlic, minced

In a small bowl, mix all ingredients until well combined.

Roll up flatware in colorful napkins, tie with ribbon bows and stack in a flat basket. Even kids can help with this well in advance... one less last-minute task!

Ham & Swiss Stromboli

Karen Wilson
Defiance, OH

A scrumptious change of pace from the traditional ham & cheese sandwich! Once you've tried this recipe, have some fun trying other combos of deli meats and cheeses.

11-oz. tube refrigerated French bread dough
3/8 lb. thinly sliced deli baked ham
6 green onions, sliced
8 slices bacon, crisply cooked and crumbled
1-1/2 c. shredded Swiss cheese
Garnish: honey mustard

Unroll dough. Layer ham slices evenly over dough to within 1/2-inch of edge. Sprinkle evenly with onions, bacon and cheese. Roll up jelly-roll style, starting on one long side. Pinch seams to seal and tuck ends under. Place seam-side down on a parchment paper-lined baking sheet. Bake, uncovered, at 350 degrees for 25 to 30 minutes, until golden and cheese is melted. Slice; serve with honey mustard. Makes 6 to 8 servings.

Spear cherry tomatoes, cheese cubes or tiny gherkin pickles with a toothpick and use to fasten mini sandwiches. Fun and tasty!

Sandwiches
for Any Occasion

Mom's Magnificent Meatballs

Julie Preston
Edwardsville, IL

Whenever we get together, my family & friends ask for these delicious meatballs. We love them on sandwiches, pasta or just as an appetizer. You can't go wrong with easy Magnificent Meatballs!

2 lbs. ground beef
1 lb. ground Italian pork sausage
1/4 c. Italian-seasoned dry bread crumbs
1/2 c. shredded Parmesan cheese
1 egg, beaten
3 T. tomato paste
1 T. dried oregano
1 T. dried basil
2 T. garlic salt
1 t. red pepper flakes
3 c. favorite pasta sauce

In a large bowl, combine all ingredients except pasta sauce. Mix until well combined. Form into golfball-size meatballs; arrange meatballs on a rimmed baking sheet. Bake, uncovered, at 400 degrees for 20 minutes, or until no longer pink in the center. Remove from oven and let stand for 10 minutes. Add pasta sauce to a large saucepan over medium heat. Add meatballs and heat through, stirring occasionally. Serve as desired. Serves 10.

An old-fashioned ice cream scoop is handy for more than just serving up frozen treats. Use it for scooping jumbo meatballs, mashed potatoes and even muffin batter...you'll have perfect portions every time!

Buffalo Chicken Wraps

Tina Wright
Atlanta, GA

My family loves chicken wings! These wraps have all their favorite flavors...great for casual meals when the kids bring home a friend or two for dinner. Just add a chopped salad and some chips.

1/2 to 1 lb. bacon
1-1/2 lbs. boneless chicken tenderloins
1 c. buffalo wing sauce, divided
8 10-inch flour tortillas, warmed
8 lettuce leaves
1 green pepper, cut into strips
1/2 c. ranch salad dressing
Optional: additional ranch dressing, celery sticks

In a large skillet over medium heat, cook bacon until crisp; set aside to drain on paper towels. Meanwhile, add chicken tenderloins and 1/2 cup sauce to another skillet over medium heat. Bring to a boil; reduce heat to medium-low. Cook for 10 to 12 minutes, stirring occasionally, until chicken juices run clear when pierced. Remove chicken from heat; cool slightly, then shred with 2 forks. To serve, top each tortilla with a lettuce leaf; spoon 1/2 cup chicken mixture down the center. Top with bacon and green pepper. Drizzle with salad dressing and remaining sauce; roll up. Garnish as desired. Makes 8 servings.

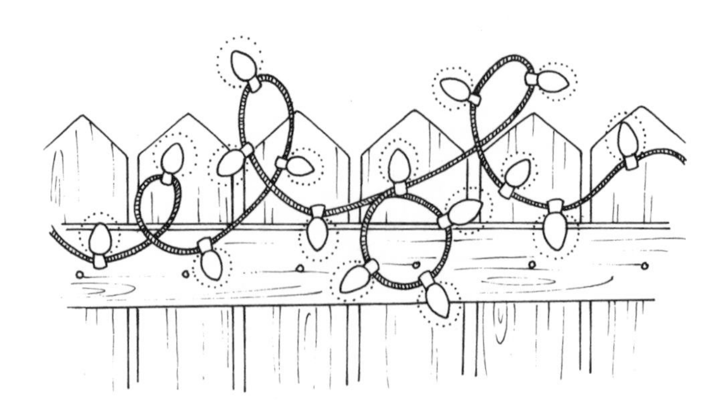

For an enchanting effect, fasten a strand of cool-burning twinkle lights to the underside of a patio table umbrella or along a fence.

Baked Tuna-Cheese Buns

Sandra Sullivan
Aurora, CO

Too busy to cook...soccer, after-school activities or just not enough minutes in the day? These make & bake buns will come to your rescue! They're good for get-togethers too...just pop in the fridge, later just bake and serve hot.

3 eggs, hard-boiled, peeled and chopped
1 to 2 6-oz. cans tuna, drained and flaked
3/4 c. American cheese, diced or shredded
1/2 c. mayonnaise
2 T. pickle relish
6 hamburger buns, split and buttered

In a bowl, combine all ingredients except buns; mix well. Spoon mixture into buns; wrap buns separately in aluminum foil. At this point, may refrigerate buns for several hours. When ready to serve, place wrapped buns on a baking sheet. Bake at 400 degrees for 10 to 15 minutes, until heated through. Makes 6 sandwiches.

Little touches make big impressions on guests, and they take just a moment. Tuck in curly parsley and cherry tomatoes on a platter of hot ham & cheese sandwiches...add bunches of grapes around sweet chicken salad croissants. Sure to be noticed!

Ham Sandwich Supreme

Carol Lytle
Columbus, OH

This easy sandwich is always welcome at potlucks, tailgating parties and other get-togethers. One sandwich will not be enough! A friend shared this recipe with me.

1 doz. brown & serve rolls, split
1/2 lb. sliced deli baked ham
12 slices provolone cheese
1/2 c. butter
2 T. brown sugar, packed
1 T. Worcestershire sauce
1 T. mustard
Optional: 1 T. poppy seed

Assemble 12 sandwiches with rolls, ham and cheese. Arrange sandwiches in a lightly buttered 13"x9" baking pan; set aside. Combine remaining ingredients in a small saucepan over medium heat. Bring to a boil, stirring until brown sugar dissolves; spoon over sandwiches. Bake, uncovered, at 350 degrees for 20 to 30 minutes, until crisp and golden on top. Makes 12 sandwiches.

Match background music to the food you're serving, to make your gathering really memorable! Check the local library for jazz, salsa or other favorites to set a lively tone...keep it low so everyone can enjoy the conversation.

Sandwiches for Any Occasion

Harvey Ham Sandwiches

Ginny Watson
Scranton, PA

The first time I tried this recipe, everyone raved about it! It's so easy to prepare, then I just set out the slow cooker and let everyone fix their own sandwiches. Serve with dill pickle slices, potato chips and coleslaw for a meal that will please everyone.

5 to 6-lb. bone-in cooked ham
8-oz. jar mustard
2 c. brown sugar, packed
24 slider rolls, split

Place ham in a 6-quart slow cooker; add enough water to partially cover. Cover and cook on low setting for 8 to 10 hours, until ham is very tender. Remove ham to a platter; cool and pull into shreds. Drain juices in slow cooker. Return shredded ham to slow cooker; stir in mustard and brown sugar. Cover and cook on low setting just until heated through. Serve ham on rolls. Makes 24 sandwiches.

Watch yard sales for a vintage salad dressing server. It's perfect for serving up a variety of mustards for ham sandwiches, from mild to spicy to super-spicy!

Tuna Croissant Sandwiches

Cheri Maxwell
Gulf Breeze, FL

This is my favorite sandwich to serve whenever my girlfriends come to visit...they love it too! Just add a fruit cup...yummy!

6.4-oz. pouch tuna, drained and flaked
3 green onions, sliced
1/2 c. dill pickles, chopped
1 stalk celery, chopped
1/2 c. mayonnaise
salt and pepper to taste
4 croissants, halved
4 tomato slices
4 leaves lettuce
Optional: 1/4 c. sliced banana peppers

In a large bowl, combine tuna, onions, pickles, celery, mayonnaise and seasonings. Mix well; spoon onto croissant bottoms. Top with tomato, lettuce, banana peppers if desired and croissant tops. Makes 4 sandwiches.

Crab Salad Croissants

Marla Kinnersley
Surprise, AZ

We're always trying to eat healthier at our house, so I came up with this delicious crab salad. It's great on wheat croissants... too good not to share with friends!

2 8-oz. pkgs. flake-style imitation crabmeat, chopped
2-1/4 oz. can sliced black olives, drained
1 stalk celery, finely chopped
2 T. red onion, finely chopped
1/4 c. light mayonnaise
juice of 1/2 lemon
1-1/2 t. ranch salad dressing mix
4 wheat croissants, split
Garnish: leafy green lettuce, sliced avocado

In a bowl, combine all ingredients except croissants and garnish. Top each croissant bottom with a lettuce slice; spread evenly with crab salad and top with avocado slices. Makes 4 sandwiches.

Friends are the family we choose for ourselves

– Edna Buchanan

Sandwiches for Any Occasion

Curry Chicken Croissants

Miranda Ching
Kaneohe, HI

The sweet-tartness of the cranberries goes well with the curry flavor in this chicken salad filling. Any kind of bread, bun or cracker can be substituted for the croissants...it's always delicious.

- 12-1/2 oz. can chicken breast, drained and flaked
- 1/2 c. mayonnaise
- 1/2 c. sweetened dried cranberries
- 1/4 c. celery, finely diced
- 1 t. curry powder, or to taste
- Optional: 1/4 c. chopped walnuts
- 6 to 8 croissants, sliced

In a bowl, combine all ingredients except croissants; blend well. Spread evenly on bottoms of croissants; add tops. Makes 6 to 8 sandwiches.

For a garden party, wrap sandwiches in pretty food-safe paper and tie with a strand of colored kitchen twine. Stack them in a favorite basket lined with a vintage tea towel...sweet!

Slow-Cooker BBQ Chicken

Joyceann Dreibelbis
Wooster, OH

An easy and delicious hot sandwich takes only a few minutes to prepare, then the slow cooker does the work for you. Tasty in warm flour tortillas as well.

4 boneless, skinless, chicken breasts
1 onion, chopped
1/2 c. barbecue sauce
1/2 c. catsup
2 T. mustard
2 T. lemon juice
2 T. pure maple syrup
2 T. Worcestershire sauce
1/2 t. chili powder
1/4 t. garlic powder
1/8 t. cayenne pepper
6 to 8 sandwich rolls, split

Add chicken to a 4-quart slow cooker; set aside. In a bowl, combine remaining ingredients except rolls. Stir until well blended; spoon over chicken. Cover and cook on low setting for 6 hours, or on high setting for 3-1/2 hours, until chicken is very tender. Remove chicken to a bowl and shred with 2 forks. Stir chicken back into mixture in slow cooker; cover and cook for 30 more minutes. To serve, spoon chicken with sauce into rolls. Makes 6 to 8 sandwiches.

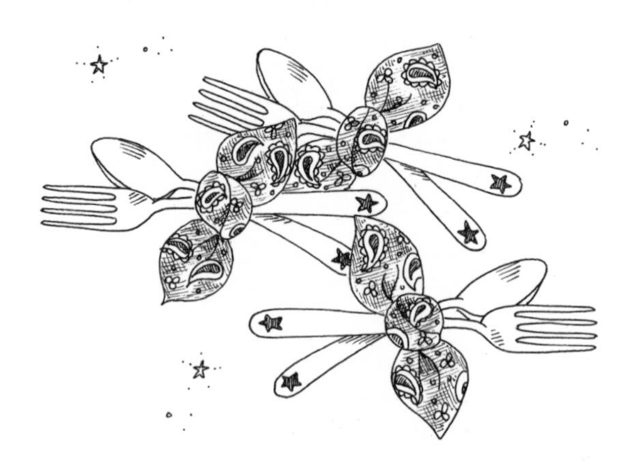

Bright-colored bandannas make colorful napkins for casual get-togethers. Tie one around each person's set of utensils. Afterwards, just toss them in the wash.

Sandwiches *for Any Occasion*

Sweet & Savory Pulled Pork

Kristin Stone
Little Elm, TX

We like this juicy pork served on a bun or stuffed into a baked potato. The roast can be cooked the day before and refrigerated, then simmered with the sauce mixture to serve hot and juicy. However you eat it, it's delicious!

3-lb. boneless pork shoulder roast
2 stalks celery, chopped
2 jalapeño peppers, chopped
14-oz. can reduced-sodium chicken broth
1/2 c. sugar
1/2 c. red wine vinegar
1/2 c. soy sauce
4 t. dry mustard
4 t. paprika
2 to 3 dashes smoke-flavored cooking sauce
12 to 16 sandwich buns, split

Place roast in a 4-quart slow cooker; top with celery and peppers. In a bowl, mix remaining ingredients except buns; spoon over roast. Cover and cook on high setting for one hour. Turn setting to low and cook for 7 hours. Remove roast from slow cooker; remove any pieces of fat and shred with 2 forks. Transfer shredded pork and all liquid from slow cooker into a large saucepan; bring to a boil over high heat. Reduce heat to low. Simmer, uncovered, for 1-1/2 hours, stirring occasionally. To serve, spoon pork mixture into buns. Makes 12 to 16 sandwiches.

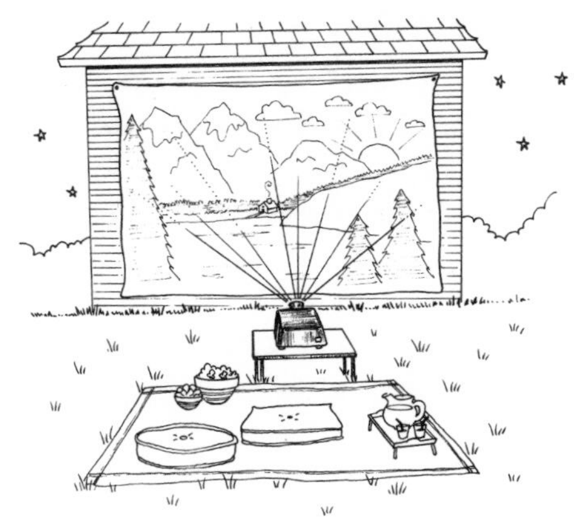

Host a movie night in your own backyard! Great fun for watching the big game together too. A local camera or rental store can set you up with everything you'll need. Sure to be a hit!

Hot Corned Beef Bagels

Kathleen DeWildt
Hudsonville, MI

I came up with this recipe back in the 80s, when I was planning a wedding shower and was looking for an inexpensive substitute for tuna or chicken. It's still a family favorite, although corned beef is no longer so inexpensive!

6 egg bagels, split
2 12-oz. cans corned beef, drained and chopped or flaked
2 T. dried, chopped onion
8-oz. pkg. shredded Cheddar cheese
1 c. mayonnaise
salt and pepper to taste

Place individual bagel halves on a baking sheet; set aside. Mix together remaining ingredients, adding mayonnaise to desired consistency. Spread mixture onto bagel halves. Bake, uncovered, at 350 degrees for 15 to 20 minutes, until heated through and cheese is bubbly. Makes 12 open-face sandwiches.

Fun polka-dotty paper napkins and matching plates make for a table that's set with whimsy...and clean-up is a breeze!

Sandwiches for Any Occasion

Card-Night Beef & Onion Spread

Eileen Bennett
Jenison, MI

A weekend card night with close friends was always looked forward to when my kids were little. At the end of the evening, these sandwiches were one of our favorite treats.

12-oz. can corned beef, drained and broken up
1 c. sour cream
2 T. onion soup mix
1 T. mayonnaise-style salad dressing
24 mini potato rolls, split

Combine all ingredients except rolls; mix well. Spread mixture into rolls; individually wrap rolls tightly in aluminum foil. Place rolls on a baking sheet. Bake at 325 degrees for 20 minutes, or until heated through. Makes 24 sandwiches.

A box of pre-cut foil squares is a big time-saver for for wrapping up a panful of baked sandwiches.

Sunshine Chicken Salad Sandwiches

Ali Crotzer
Huntsville, AL

I grew up loving my mom's chicken salad sandwiches so much, I served them at my wedding luncheon! Since then, I've added to the recipe and it's become my favorite lunch.

- 2 12-1/2 oz. cans white chicken, drained and flaked
- 1-1/2 c. celery, chopped
- 1 c. Gala or Honeycrisp apple, cored and chopped
- 1/4 c. green onions, chopped
- 1/2 c. mayonnaise
- 1 T. Creole or other mild coarse-grained mustard
- salt and pepper to taste
- 1 c. seedless grapes, halved
- 11-oz. can mandarin oranges, drained and chopped
- 1/2 c. chopped pecans
- 6 split croissants or 12 slices toasted bread

Combine chicken, celery, apple and onions in a large bowl; set aside. In a small bowl, whisk together mayonnaise and mustard; add to chicken mixture and toss to combine. Season with salt and pepper. Cover and chill for several hours, or up to 2 days. Just before serving, gently stir in grapes, oranges and pecans. Serve on croissants or toasted bread. Makes 6 sandwiches.

A single big blossom floating in a water-filled teacup is a charming touch for a ladies' lunch. Set one at each guest's place...sweet!

Sandwiches *for Any Occasion*

Special Egg Salad

Marsha Baker
Pioneer, OH

Many agree with me, this is the best egg salad you'll ever taste. It's scrumptious served on sandwiches or with crackers... or simply enjoyed with a fork!

6 eggs, hard-boiled and peeled
1/2 c. cream cheese, softened
1/4 c. mayonnaise or mayonnaise-style salad dressing
1/2 t. sugar
1/4 t. onion powder
1/4 t. garlic powder
1/8 t. salt
1/8 t. pepper
12 slices wheat bread, toasted
Garnish: lettuce leaves

Chop eggs and set aside in a large bowl. In a small bowl, beat cream cheese until smooth. Stir in mayonnaise or salad dressing, sugar and seasonings; add to eggs and mix gently. Cover and refrigerate for one hour before serving. Spread mixture on 6 slices toasted bread; top with lettuce and remaining bread. Makes 6 sandwiches.

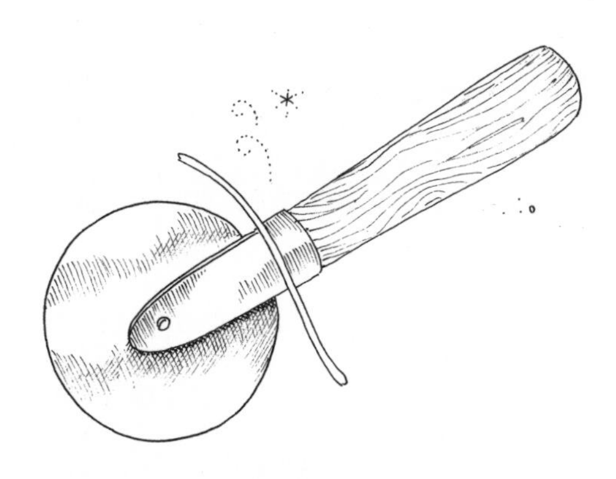

A pizza cutter makes quick work of cutting the crusts off slices of bread for crustless sandwiches.

BBQ Oven Hot Dogs

Kathy Courington
Canton, GA

My hubby loves hot dogs fixed this way! Tasty with a side of coleslaw and some crispy French fries.

1 lb. hot dogs
1/2 c. catsup
1/4 c. onion, minced
2 t. white vinegar
2 t. water
1-1/2 t. Worcestershire sauce
1 t. all-purpose flour
1 t. brown sugar, packed
1 t. paprika
1 t. chili powder
2 t. salt
1/4 t. pepper
Optional: 8 hot dog buns, split and toasted

Pierce each hot dog several times with a fork; arrange in a greased 13"x9" baking pan. Combine remaining ingredients in a bowl; spoon over hot dogs. Cover and bake at 350 degrees for one hour. Serve hot dogs on toasted buns, or as is. Makes 8 servings.

BBQ Pickled Onions

Staci Prickett
Montezuma, GA

These zesty onions will take your BBQ to the next level! They are great on hamburgers, hot dogs, pulled pork and barbecue baked beans. For extra kick, try adding a small jalapeño. If mustard-based barbecue sauce isn't your thing, try your favorite tomato-based sauce and simply omit the brown sugar.

2 large sweet onions, halved if desired and thinly sliced
1 c. cider vinegar
1 c. tangy mustard-based barbecue sauce
1/4 c. dark brown sugar, packed

Pack sliced onions in a one-quart canning jar; set aside. In a bowl, whisk together remaining ingredients until brown sugar dissolves. Spoon mixture over onions in jar. Cover and refrigerate at least 3 days before serving, to allow onions to pickle. Makes 15 to 20 servings.

Quick & Easy Dill Mustard

Eileen Bennett
Jenison, MI

Nothing tastes better than a sandwich made with homemade mustard! Our guys especially like the tasty tang of this recipe. The ingredients can easily be halved for a trial run of this recipe.

1 c. dry mustard
1 c. cider vinegar
1/4 c. water
3/4 c. sugar
2 T. fresh dill weed, finely chopped
2 t. salt
2 eggs, lightly beaten

In a large bowl, combine all ingredients except eggs; stir well. Cover and refrigerate for 4 to 6 hours. Pour mixture into the top of a double boiler; warm gently over medium heat. Stir in eggs. Cook and stir over medium-low heat for about 10 minutes, until thickened. Pour into a covered container and chill; keep refrigerated. Makes 1-1/2 cups.

Easiest-ever sandwiches for a get-together...a big platter of deli cold cuts and cheese, a basket of fresh breads and a choice of condiments so guests can make their own. Add some chips and pickles...done!

Reuben Sliders

Lisa Rischar
Crestwood, IL

Quick, easy and delicious. Just add some chips and a pickle spear!

12-oz. pkg. Hawaiian sweet rolls
1/3 c. Thousand Island salad dressing
1/2 lb. sliced Swiss cheese, divided
1 c. sauerkraut, well drained
1/2 lb. sliced deli corned beef
1/4 c. butter, melted
1 T. Dijon mustard
1/2 t. garlic powder
1 t. dried, minced onion

Slice package of rolls in half horizontally; place bottom half in a lightly greased 13"x9" baking pan. Spread salad dressing over rolls in pan; layer with half of cheese slices, all of sauerkraut, all of corned beef and remaining cheese. Add tops of rolls. Stir together remaining ingredients in a cup; brush over rolls. Bake, uncovered, at 350 degrees for 20 to 25 minutes, until heated through and cheese is melted. Makes 12 sliders.

Make clean-up easy by lining your wastebasket with 3 or 4 disposal bags. No need to find more bags mid-party!

Spicy Sliders

Beth Flack
Terre Haute, IN

Make these for an easy, quick school night dinner, tailgating party or appetizer at Christmas. This makes two pans, enough for a hungry crowd! But it's simple to halve the recipe for a smaller gathering.

1 lb. hot ground pork sausage
1 lb. ground beef chuck
2 10-oz. cans diced tomatoes with green chiles
16-oz. pkg. pasteurized process cheese, cubed
24 slider buns, split
1/4 c. butter, melted

Cook sausage and beef in a large skillet over medium heat, stirring until crumbled and no longer pink. Drain well; add tomatoes with juice and cheese. Cook for about 8 minutes, stirring often, until well blended and cheese is melted. Arrange bottom halves of 12 buns in each of 2 lightly greased 13"x9" baking pans. Spoon sausage mixture onto bun bottoms; add bun tops. Brush buns with melted butter. Bake, uncovered, at 350 degrees for about 12 minutes, until heated through. Makes 2 dozen.

Choose sturdy sectional paper plates...no more baked beans running into the potato chips! Or pick up a stack of colorful plastic ones that can be used again & again. Guests are sure to appreciate it.

Picnic-Pleaser Sandwich Loaf

Dale Duncan
Waterloo, IA

This giant sandwich has become a family tradition...we love to try out different meats and cheese from the deli! It's a must for any picnic occasion. Sometimes, instead of the olive oil, we brush mayonnaise and/or mustard over the cut sides of the loaf. Any way you make it, it's a hit!

1-1/4 lb. round bread loaf, sliced in half horizontally
1/4 c. olive oil, divided
3/4 lb. thinly sliced deli baked ham
1/2 lb. thinly sliced Genoa salami
1/2 lb. thinly sliced provolone cheese
1 to 2 tomatoes, thinly sliced
2 c. lettuce, shredded
3 T. red wine vinegar
salt and pepper to taste

Pull out some of the soft bread inside both halves of loaf, removing more from the bottom half than the top. Brush cut sides of each half with one tablespoon olive oil. On bottom half of loaf, layer ham, salami and cheese; top with tomatoes and lettuce. Drizzle lettuce with vinegar and remaining oil; season with salt and pepper. Add top half of loaf; press down lightly. Tightly double-wrap in plastic wrap; refrigerate for one to 8 hours. To serve, unwrap sandwich and cut into wedges with a long serrated knife. Serves 8 to 10.

Fill a 6-pack beverage container with utensils and rolled-up napkins... easy to tote to the picnic table.

Sensational Salads & Sides

Aunt Judy's Baked Macaroni & Cheese

Judy Croll
Rowlett, TX

My family always requests this comforting dish for special holiday gatherings. It is so simple to prepare, and delicious with baked ham or just by itself. There are never any leftovers.

8-oz. pkg. elbow macaroni, uncooked
2 T. oil
1 T. plus 1 t. salt, divided
1/4 c. butter
1/3 c. all-purpose flour
3 c. milk, warmed
1/2 t. pepper
8-oz. pkg. pasteurized process cheese, cubed
1/2 c. shredded Cheddar cheese

Cook macaroni according to package directions, adding oil and one tablespoon salt to cooking water; drain and set aside. Meanwhile, melt butter in a large saucepan over medium heat. Add flour; cook and stir for 3 minutes, or until bubbly. Do not brown. Whisk in warm milk and bring to a boil, stirring constantly. Add remaining salt, pepper and cubed cheese. Stir until cheese is melted; remove from heat. Add cooked macaroni to cheese sauce and stir. Transfer to a buttered 2-quart casserole dish. Bake, uncovered, at 350 degrees for 20 to 30 minutes, until bubbly. Top with shredded cheese; return to oven just until cheese melts. Serves 8 to 10.

Start a tradition of having a regular night for guests at dinner. Invite a new neighbor or a co-worker you've wanted to get to know better... encourage your kids to invite a friend. You'll be so glad you did!

Heavenly Onion Casserole

Emilie Britton
New Bremen, OH

This is amazingly delicious! A wonderful addition to a meal.

2 T. butter
3 sweet onions, sliced
1/2 lb. sliced mushrooms
1 c. shredded Swiss cheese
10-3/4 oz. can cream of mushroom soup
5-oz. can evaporated milk
2 t. soy sauce
6 to 8 slices French bread
6 to 8 slices Swiss cheese

Melt butter in a large skillet over medium heat. Sauté onions and mushrooms until tender; transfer to a greased 2-quart casserole dish. Sprinkle with shredded cheese; set aside. In a bowl, whisk together soup, milk and soy sauce; spoon over cheese. Top with bread slices; arrange cheese slices over bread. Cover loosely and bake at 375 degrees for 30 minutes. Uncover; bake another 15 minutes. Let stand for 5 minutes before serving. Serves 6 to 8.

Barbecued Green Beans

Zoe Bennett
Columbia, SC

The tangy flavor makes these beans a great side with grilled meats. It's all done on the stovetop...convenient when the oven is in use.

4 slices bacon, chopped
1/4 c. white vinegar
1/2 c. sugar
1/2 c. brown sugar, packed
4 14-1/2 oz. cans green beans
salt and pepper to taste

In a large saucepan over medium heat, cook bacon until crisp. Remove bacon to paper towels; drain pan. Add vinegar and sugars to same pan; bring to a boil over medium heat. Add 2 undrained cans of beans to pan; drain remaining beans and add. Stir in crumbled bacon; season with salt and pepper. Bring to a boil over medium heat; reduce heat to medium-low. Simmer for about 20 minutes, stirring occasionally, until sauce is thickened and flavors have blended, about 20 minutes. Serves 8.

Farmers' Market Roasted Veggies

*Sheila Peregrin
Lancaster, PA*

I've been making some variation of this side dish for nearly 40 years. It also makes a great appetizer. Just roast the vegetables, arrange everything on a lovely platter and let people forage for favorites while they sip a beverage and socialize...delicious!

- 3 to 4 c. assorted vegetables, peeled and sliced, like potatoes, carrots, sweet peppers, zucchini, yellow squash and onions
- 1/4 c. olive oil
- 1 T. lemon juice
- 3 cloves garlic, minced
- salt and pepper to taste

Combine all ingredients in a large plastic zipping bag; toss to mix well. Spread vegetables on greased baking sheets. Bake at 425 degrees for 30 minutes; stir. Check for doneness. Bake for another 5 to 15 minutes, or until fork-tender. Serves 6.

For special-occasion menus, tried & true is best! Use simple recipes you know will be a hit, rather than trying new recipes at the last minute. Everyone will be happy, and you'll avoid tossing dishes that didn't turn out as expected.

Comfy Cheese Potatoes

Krista LaFave
Roseville, MI

This is a family favorite for all get-togethers...and it goes together quickly! You can change this up with different types of cheeses such Asiago or Havarti for a new flavor.

32-oz. pkg. frozen potato puffs, thawed
8-oz. container sour cream
1/2 c. butter, melted
8-oz. pkg. shredded mild Cheddar cheese, divided
8-oz. pkg. shredded Monterey Jack cheese, divided
Optional: 1 c. chopped onions and/or 1 c. crisply cooked and crumbled bacon

Break up thawed potato puffs into a large bowl. Add sour cream and melted butter; stir well. Add 3/4 of each cheese and optional ingredients if desired; mix again. Spoon mixture into a lightly greased 13"x9" baking pan; spread evenly. Spread remaining cheeses on top; cover with aluminum foil. Bake at 350 degrees for 45 minutes, or until bubbly and golden. Makes 8 servings.

A sprinkle of paprika makes any baked potato dish look even more appealing.

Blitzburgh Beans

Staci Prickett
Montezuma, GA

A favorite tailgating side of ours...give it a try, and it's sure to become yours too!

1/2 lb. ground beef
1/2 lb. Kielbasa sausage, sliced into 1-inch pieces
1/2 lb. bacon, sliced into 1-inch pieces
1/2 c. onion, chopped
1/2 c. green pepper, chopped
3/4 c. brown sugar, packed
1/2 c. catsup
salt and pepper to taste
2 16-oz. cans pork & beans
2 15-1/2 oz. cans kidney beans
2 15-1/2 oz. cans butter beans

In a large skillet over medium heat, brown together beef, sausage and bacon; drain. Add onion and green pepper; cook until slightly tender. Stir in brown sugar, catsup, salt and pepper. Add all beans; do not drain cans. Mix well. Transfer to a greased 13"x9" baking pan. Bake, uncovered, at 350 degrees for 40 to 50 minutes, until hot and bubbly. Makes 8 to 12 servings.

At buffets, guests will appreciate table-tent cards labeling the dishes, so they can easily see what is in each one before they dig in. Mini chalkboard signs are easy and fun too.

Mrs. Miller's Corn Soufflé

Lauren Williams
Mayfield, KY

This dish is delicious and so different. A dear lady at church served this dish at many functions...it was a favorite of ours. She is deeply missed, but now I bake it to honor her memory.

2 15-1/4 oz. cans yellow corn, drained and divided
4 c. milk
3/4 c. cornmeal
15-oz. can white shoepeg corn, drained
2 4-oz. cans diced green chiles, drained
2 eggs, beaten
1-1/2 t. chili powder
1 t. salt
1/2 t. pepper

In a food processor, purée one can yellow corn; set aside. Heat milk in a large saucepan over medium heat until very hot. Stir in cornmeal; cook and stir for 5 minutes, or until thickened. Stir in puréed and whole yellow corn, shoepeg corn, chiles, eggs and seasonings. Pour mixture into a buttered 2-quart casserole or soufflé dish. Bake, uncovered, at 350 degrees for about one hour and 10 minutes, until set and golden. Makes 8 servings.

Host a firepit get-together in the fall, when the weather turns cool and crisp. Set out weenies for roasting...add a hearty pot of baked beans, simmering spiced cider to drink and later, s'mores for dessert. What fun!

Quick & Easy Recipes for Gatherings

Potluck Potato Casserole

Sharon Beaty
Boonville, IN

This is a family favorite and a crowd-pleaser at carry-in dinners. It is very easy to make and goes with everything! I love to make it when it gets cool outdoors...the oven warms our kitchen.

8 russet potatoes, scrubbed
2 10-3/4 oz. cans cream of chicken soup
1/4 c. plus 2 T. butter, melted and divided
1/2 c. sour cream
1/2 c. shredded Cheddar cheese
2 c. corn flake cereal, crushed

Pierce potatoes with a fork. Bake at 350 degrees for 60 minutes, or until fork-tender. Cool, peel and grate potatoes; transfer to a bowl. Add soup, 1/4 cup melted butter, sour cream and cheese; mix well. Spoon mixture into a greased 13"x9" baking pan. Toss crushed cereal with remaining butter; sprinkle on top. Bake, uncovered, at 350 degrees for 30 minutes, or until hot and bubbly. Serves 10 to 12.

Mom Woodring's Baked Beans

Julie Woodring
Ramey, PA

My mother-in-law created this delicious dish. It's been a staple at every family gathering and Sunday School picnic for many years.

2 24-oz. cans baked beans
1/4 c. sugar
1/4 c. brown sugar, packed
1/4 c. catsup
1/4 c. mustard
1 lb. bacon, chopped

Mix all ingredients together; transfer to a greased 2-quart casserole dish. Bake at 350 degrees for 1-1/2 hours, stirring every 30 minutes. May also transfer to a slow cooker; cover with the lid set slightly ajar and cook on high setting for 3 hours, stirring once every hour. Makes 10 to 12 servings.

Set out some stick-on labels and a waterproof pen so guests can label their potluck containers.

Corny Green Bean Casserole

Cindy Neel
Gooseberry Patch

This recipe is my old standby for cookouts and potlucks. Everyone seems to like it...even the ones who don't like vegetables!

- 16-oz. pkg. frozen French-style green beans, thawed and drained
- 2 c. frozen corn, thawed and drained
- 10-3/4 oz. can cream of celery soup
- 1 c. onion, chopped
- 8-oz. container sour cream
- 1 c. shredded Cheddar cheese
- salt and pepper to taste
- 1-1/2 c. buttery round crackers, crushed
- 1/2 c. French fried onions, coarsely crushed

Combine all ingredients except crackers and French fried onions in a large bowl; mix well. Spread evenly in a greased 13"x9" baking pan; sprinkle with crushed crackers and French fried onions. Bake, uncovered, at 350 degrees for 25 to 35 minutes, until bubbly and golden. Makes 8 servings.

To protect a wooden table top from spills, cover it with several layers of newspaper before covering with a tablecloth.

3-Pepper Confetti Rice

Victoria Mitchel
Gettysburg, PA

When I got a great deal on sweet peppers at our local farm market, I came up with this recipe for a Mexican potluck at church. As I added this & that, I jotted down the ingredients and measurements. I'm so glad I did! My husband, kids and I couldn't stop eating it. Luckily, most of it still made it to the potluck!

1 to 2 T. olive oil
1 green pepper, diced
1 red pepper, diced
1 orange pepper, diced
2 c. long-grain rice, uncooked
10-oz. can diced tomatoes with green chiles
4 c. water
1 t. chili lime seasoning or regular chili powder
1/2 t. smoked paprika
1/2 t. kosher salt
1/2 t. dried oregano
1/4 t. garlic powder
Optional: lime slices, fresh cilantro

Heat olive oil in a large saucepan over medium heat; add peppers and sauté until softened. Add uncooked rice; cook and stir until rice starts to turn golden. Add tomatoes with juices, water and seasonings; bring to a boil. Reduce heat to medium-low. Cover and cook about 15 minutes, until liquid is almost completely absorbed, Turn burner off; let pan stand on burner for 10 to 15 minutes. Uncover; fluff with a fork. Serve with slices of lime and fresh cilantro, if desired. Makes 10 to 12 servings.

For special occasions, set out a guest book alongside a jar filled with colored pens. Encourage everyone to sign it...even small kids can draw a picture! Add favorite photos and you'll have a cherished scrapbook in no time.

Cheesy Noodle Casserole

Ruth Cooksey
Plainfield, IN

We just love these extra-cheesy noodles...everyone else who has tried them does too!

16-oz. pkg. wide egg noodles, uncooked
16-oz. container cottage cheese
10-3/4 oz. can Cheddar soup
1 c. half-and-half
1 c. shredded Cheddar cheese
8-oz. pkg. cream cheese, cubed
2 T. butter
salt and pepper to taste
1/2 c. shredded Parmesan cheese
3/4 c. salad croutons, crushed

Cook noodles according to package directions; drain. Combine noodles and cottage cheese in a lightly greased 13"x9" baking pan; mix gently and set aside. In a saucepan, combine soup, half-and-half, Cheddar cheese, cream cheese and butter. Cook and stir over medium heat until blended and cheeses and butter are melted. Season with salt and pepper; spoon over noodle mixture. Sprinkle with Parmesan cheese and crushed croutons. Bake, uncovered, at 350 degrees for 12 to 15 minutes, until bubbly and golden. Serves 8.

No need to scrub the stubborn baked-on cheese left in the casserole dish... try this! Fill the dish with warm water and add a couple teaspoons of baking soda. Let stand overnight. The next day, the baked-on portion will loosen easily.

Nonna's Italian-Style Potato Salad

Sharon Velenosi
Costa Mesa, CA

This recipe was so well loved by the family, my Nonna made it often. It's good with chicken or any kind of meat. Our favorite was when she served it with homemade meatball sandwiches. Nonna's tip...the potatoes are done when you can poke them with a small knife and they drop right off!

- 1 lb. new redskin potatoes
- 1 to 2 ripe tomatoes, coarsely diced
- 1 red onion, sliced
- 2 T. capers, drained
- 1/4 c. pitted Kalamata olives, chopped
- 1/4 c. fresh parsley, chopped
- 2 eggs, hard-boiled and peeled
- 1/2 c. extra-virgin olive oil
- 1/4 c. seasoned rice vinegar
- 1/8 t. dried oregano
- 1/8 t. granulated garlic
- salt and pepper to taste

In a large saucepan, cover potatoes with water; bring to a boil over high heat. Simmer until potatoes are tender, about 20 to 30 minutes, until pierced easily with a knife tip. Drain; rinse with cold water to cool. Cut potatoes into chunks and place in a large bowl. Add tomatoes, onion, capers, olives and parsley; toss well. Cut hard-boiled eggs into slices or wedges and arrange on top; set aside. In a small bowl, whisk together remaining ingredients; drizzle over salad. Best served at room temperature. Serves 10 to 12.

Whether it's Fiesta Night, 1950s Diner or Hawaiian Luau, a creative theme suggests appropriate foods, decorations and music. It gives everyone something fun on their calendars to look forward to!

Sensational Salads & Sides

Connie's Cucumber Salad

Connie Wagner
Manchester, PA

Made with love and mayonnaise!

2 cucumbers, peeled and thinly sliced
1/2 c. onion, thinly sliced
1 c. mayonnaise
1/4 c. buttermilk
1/4 c. sugar
4 t. vinegar
1/2 t. dried dill weed
1/8 t. salt
1/8 t. pepper

Combine all ingredients in a large bowl; stir well. Cover and refrigerate for 8 hours, or overnight. Stir again before serving. Serves 8 to 10.

Italian Veggie Salad

Diana Krol
Hutchinson, KS

This salad is really good served with barbecued meats on the grill and fried chicken. Especially good using garden-fresh tomatoes in the summer!

1 bunch broccoli, cut into bite-size flowerets
1 head cauliflower, cut into bite-size flowerets
1 pt. grape tomatoes
1 pt. small mushrooms, trimmed
8-oz. bottle favorite Italian salad dressing

In a large bowl, combine all vegetables. Add desired amount of salad dressing; stir gently. Cover and refrigerate for 4 hours or overnight, stirring occasionally. Serves 10 to 12.

Now and then, it's good to pause in our pursuit of happiness and just be happy.
– Guillaume Apollinaire

Delicious Layered Vegetable Salad

Judy Smith
Bellevue, WA

A favorite for holiday gatherings! It's an easy make-ahead that everyone loves...goes with all kinds of main dishes and sandwiches.

- 1 head iceberg lettuce, torn into bite-size pieces
- 1 c. celery, chopped
- 3 green onions, chopped
- 8-oz. can water chestnuts, drained and chopped
- 10-oz. pkg. frozen peas
- 2 c. mayonnaise
- 1-1/2 T. sugar
- 1 c. grated Parmesan cheese
- 1 c. real bacon bits

Spread lettuce in a 13"x9" clear glass baking pan. Layer as follows: celery, onions, water chestnuts and frozen peas. Set aside. In a bowl, stir together mayonnaise and sugar. Spoon over top of salad, covering well. Sprinkle with Parmesan cheese and bacon bits. Cover and refrigerate for 8 hours or overnight before serving. Serves 10 to 12.

Tuck family photos on wire picks into a floral arrangement... a clever conversation starter for get-togethers.

Sensational Salads & Sides

Greek Tomato & Cucumber Salad

Donna Carter
Ontario, Canada

A tasty recipe that I received from a co-worker years ago...I have added a few more ingredients to make my own. It's delicious. Just toss everything together a day ahead and tuck it in the fridge.

2 c. cucumbers, chopped
2 tomatoes, cut into chunks
1/2 c. green pepper, coarsely chopped
1/2 c. red onion, thinly sliced
1/4 c. crumbled feta cheese
Optional: 1/4 c. sliced black or green olives
1/2 c. Greek vinaigrette salad dressing with feta & oregano

Toss all ingredients in a serving bowl. For the best flavor, cover and refrigerate for 8 hours or overnight before serving. Serves 4 to 6.

Celery Seed Coleslaw

Robin Hill
Rochester, NY

Great for topping sandwiches, or serve on its own...very tasty!

3 c. shredded coleslaw mix
2 T. green onions, thinly sliced
2 T. mayonnaise
1-1/2 t. white vinegar
1 t. sugar
1/2 t. celery seed
1/4 t. salt
1/4 t. pepper

Combine all ingredients in a large bowl; toss to mix well. Cover and chill until serving time. Makes 6 servings.

Add a homemade touch to prepared wild rice mix...simply stir in some diced, sautéed mushrooms, onions or celery.

Strawberry-Romaine Salad

Patricia Alfrey
Independence, MO

I got this delectable recipe from a coworker, who served it at a Christmas potluck dinner. Since making it for my family, it is the most-requested salad at our family gatherings!

2 heads romaine lettuce, torn into bite-size pieces
1 pt. strawberries, hulled and sliced
1 red onion, chopped
1/2 c. chopped pecans, toasted
1 c. favorite shredded cheese

Combine lettuce, strawberries, onion and pecans in a large bowl; toss to mix. Pour Dressing over salad and toss again; cover and refrigerate. Add cheese before serving. Serves 10.

Dressing:

3/4 c. oil
3/4 c. sugar
1/2 c. red wine vinegar
2 cloves garlic, minced
1/2 t. paprika
1/2 t. salt
1/4 t. pepper

Combine all ingredients in a jar with a lid. Cover and shake well.

Hosting a shower for a bride-to-be or a new mother? Drape the guest of honor's chair with pastel netting & ribbon. She'll feel like Queen for a Day!

Mom's Cornbread Salad

Priscilla Caskey Howard
Morehead, KY

My mother gave me this recipe. This dish is delicious and perfect for sharing...beautiful when served in a big glass punch bowl!

- 2 8-1/2 oz. pkgs. corn muffin mix
- 1 head iceberg lettuce, chopped
- 1 head cauliflower, chopped
- 5 tomatoes, diced
- 1 green pepper, chopped
- 6 green onions, chopped
- 16-oz. jar mayonnaise
- 1 c. shredded Cheddar cheese
- 1 c. shredded mozzarella cheese
- 7 slices bacon, crisply cooked and crumbled

Prepare corn muffin mix and bake in a 13"x9" baking pan, according to package directions. Set aside to cool. In a large bowl, combine all vegetables. Add mayonnaise; mix well and set aside. Crumble half of cornbread into a large glass bowl. Layer with half of vegetable mixture; repeat layering. Layer with Cheddar cheese, mozzarella cheese and crumbled bacon. Cover and chill until serving time. Serves 10 to 15.

Here's a tip for any buffet table...stack your plates at the beginning, but save the flatware, napkins and beverages for the end of the line. So much easier to handle!

Blue-Ribbon Broccoli Salad

Eileen Bennett
Jenison, MI

This oh-so-delicious salad was served at a Christmas luncheon back in the early 1980s. It is still a year 'round family favorite, almost 40 years later.

2 bunches broccoli, cut into bite-sized pieces
2 lbs. sliced mushrooms
4 green onions, including a bit of the tops, sliced

Combine all vegetables in a large bowl. Drizzle with Dressing and toss to coat. Cover and refrigerate for 2 hours before serving. Makes 12 servings.

Dressing:

1 c. olive oil or salad oil
1/4 c. white vinegar
1/2 c. sugar
1 t. paprika
1 t. celery seed
1 t. salt
Optional: 1 t. onion powder

Combine all ingredients in a bowl; beat with an electric mixer on low speed until well blended.

Paint guests' names on clear glass tealight holders with acrylic paint. Drop in a tealight candle, then set lit candles at place settings... a welcoming glow and a sweet table favor.

Fresh Fruit Salad

JoAnn
Gooseberry Patch

Gorgeous colors...serve in your prettiest cut-glass bowl, or serve up picnic-style in a hollowed-out watermelon!

1-1/2 pts. fresh strawberries, hulled and halved
1-1/2 c. fresh raspberries
1-1/2 c. fresh blueberries
2 navel oranges, peeled and sectioned
1-1/2 c. honeydew melon balls
3/4 c. orange juice
1/2 c. honey
1/3 c. fresh mint, chopped

Combine all fruits in a large bowl; set aside. Whisk together juice and honey; pour over fruit. Sprinkle with mint. Cover and chill at least one hour before serving. Makes 8 servings.

Keep cool salads chilled. Simply nestle the salad serving bowl into a larger bowl filled with crushed ice.

Bacon-Cheddar Coleslaw

Susan Jacobs
Vista, CA

One 4th of July, I wanted to jazz up my coleslaw. We'd been on a low-carb diet and we liked the coleslaw mix sautéed with bacon, so we gave it a try all chilled together. It's yummy!

3/4 lb. bacon, cut into 1-inch pieces
1 c. mayonnaise
2 T. Dijon mustard
2 T. white vinegar
1/2 t. salt
1/2 t. pepper
Optional: 1 to 2 T. milk
16-oz. pkg. tri-color shredded coleslaw mix
8-oz. pkg. shredded Cheddar cheese, divided
1/4 c. green onions, chopped

Cook bacon in a skillet over medium heat until crisp. Using a slotted spoon, remove bacon to a paper towel-lined plate. Set aside 3 tablespoons bacon drippings to cool. In a bowl, combine mayonnaise, mustard, vinegar, salt, pepper and reserved drippings. If too thick, thin with a little milk to a salad dressing consistency; set aside. In a large bowl, toss together coleslaw mix, half of cheese and half of bacon. Pour dressing over coleslaw and toss to coat. Sprinkle with remaining cheese, bacon and onions. Cover and chill for 2 hours before serving. Serves 8 to 10.

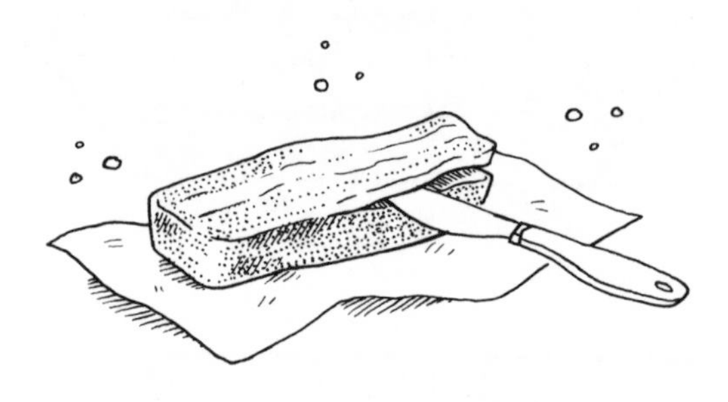

Need to chop a package of bacon? Unwrap and cut across the slices while still in one block. The pieces will separate as they fry.

Southwestern Wheat Berry Salad

*Liz Plotnick-Snay
Gooseberry Patch*

My husband and I enjoy making and sharing this salad. For variety, I've made it replacing the chiles, peppers, red onion & black beans with yellow & green zucchini, fresh tomatoes, green onions and garbanzo beans...just as good! You'll want to prepare the wheat berries ahead of time.

3/4 c. wheat berries, uncooked
2 Anaheim chiles, roasted and chopped
15-1/2 oz. can black beans, drained and rinsed
1 c. green pepper, diced
1 c. red pepper, diced
1/2 c. red onion, minced
2 cloves garlic, minced
3 T. lime juice
1-1/2 T. olive oil
1/4 t. salt

Place wheat berries in a saucepan; add enough water to cover by 2 inches. Cover saucepan and let stand for 8 hours; drain. Cover berries with 2 inches fresh water. Bring to a boil; reduce heat and simmer, uncovered, for one hour or until tender. Drain and set aside. Prepare Roasted Chiles. In a large bowl, combine berries, chiles and remaining ingredients. Serve at room temperature or chilled. Serves 6 to 8.

Roasted Chiles: Cut 2 Anaheim chiles in half lengthwise; discard seeds. Place chile halves, skin-side up, on an aluminum foil-lined baking sheet; press flat. Broil chiles for 8 minutes, or until blackened. Transfer chiles to a heavy-duty plastic zipping bag. Seal and let stand for 10 minutes. Peel chiles and chop.

Ripe red tomatoes from the farmers' market are such a treat. Serve them simply, with just a dash of oil & vinegar and a sprinkle of fresh basil.

Ray's Apple Slaw

Donna Carter
Ontario, Canada

I have adapted this recipe over the years. I call it Ray's because this is my husband's favorite salad, although he is not really a salad eater. Easy to prepare and can be made the day before to let the flavors blend. Scrumptious!

- 3/4 c. light mayonnaise-style salad dressing
- 1 T. honey
- 12-oz. pkg. shredded coleslaw mix
- 1 red Cortland or Jonathan apple, cored and cubed
- 1 green Granny Smith apple, cored and cubed
- 3 slices bacon, crisply cooked and crumbled
- 1/4 c. onion, chopped
- 1/4 c. broccoli, chopped
- 1/4 c. carrot, peeled and chopped
- 1/4 c. celery, peeled and chopped
- 1/4 c. sweetened dried cranberries

Stir together dressing and honey in a large bowl until blended. Add remaining ingredients; mix lightly. Cover and refrigerate for one hour or overnight before serving. Serves 10 to 12.

Keep chilled salads cold...oh-so easy! Pop a stoneware bowl into the freezer, then at serving time, spoon salad into the chilled bowl. The salad will stay fresh and crisp.

Orzo Fruit Salad

Marcia Marcoux
Charlton, MA

A great dish for a large gathering...it's sure to please everyone! I like to add a pint of fresh blueberries for added taste and interest.

20-oz. can pineapple chunks, drained and juice reserved
20-oz. can crushed pineapple, drained and juice reserved
2 15-oz. cans mandarin oranges, drained and juice reserved
4-oz. jar maraschino cherries, drained and halved
3/4 c. sugar
2 eggs, beaten
3 T. all-purpose flour
16-oz. pkg. orzo pasta, uncooked
16-oz. container frozen whipped topping, thawed
Optional: 1 pt. blueberries

In a saucepan over low heat, combine all reserved fruit juices, sugar, eggs and flour. Cook and stir until thickened, about 5 to 10 minutes. Remove from heat; cool for 30 to 60 minutes. Meanwhile, cook pasta according to package directions; drain and rinse with cold water. In a large bowl, combine cooked pasta, pineapple, oranges and cherries to pasta; mix gently. Pour cooled sauce over fruit mixture and toss to coat. Cover and refrigerate until flavors blend, 8 hours or overnight. At serving time, fold in whipped topping and optional blueberries, if using. Serves 18 to 20.

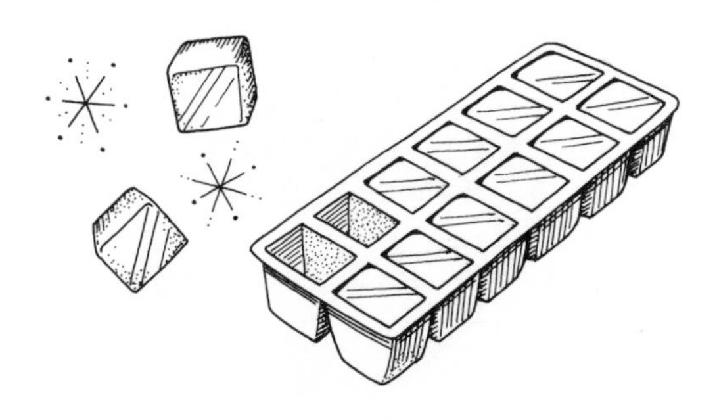

When draining canned fruit, don't toss the juice! Pour it into ice cube trays and freeze...handy for adding a little sweetness to marinades and dressings.

Minestrone Pasta Salad

Pamela Newcomer
Deltona, FL

Love this pasta salad! It's chock-full of tasty ingredients like tomatoes, pepperoni, kidney beans and tangy dressing. Perfect for picnics on hot days, since there's no mayonnaise. Easy to make!

- 12-oz. pkg. bow-tie pasta, uncooked
- 15-1/2 oz. can kidney beans, drained and rinsed
- 4 to 5 roma tomatoes, seeded and chopped
- 3-1/2 oz. pkg. sliced pepperoni
- 1/2 c. cubanelle or green pepper, seeded and chopped
- 1/4 c. fresh Italian flat-leaf parsley, chopped
- 1/4 c. shredded Parmesan cheese
- 1-1/2 t. to 1 T. fresh oregano, chopped
- pepper to taste
- 8-oz. bottle Italian vinaigrette salad dressing

Cook pasta according to package directions; drain and rinse with cold water. In a large bowl, combine cooked pasta and remaining ingredients except salad dressing; mix well. Add desired amount of salad dressing; toss to coat. Serve immediately, or cover and refrigerate until serving time. Makes 10 to 12 servings.

Treat your friends like family and your family like friends.

–John C. Maxwell

Redus Ranch Pasta Salad

Donna Henry
Medway, MA

I first tasted this salad at a high-school graduation party for my friend Anita's nephew. She had made a couple of different salads for the occasion, and I just loved this one! I often will bring this to a summer gathering...it is so refreshing and different. The flavor is best if made a day in advance.

16-oz. pkg. rotini pasta, uncooked
2 small bunches broccoli, chopped
1 c. carrots, peeled and shredded
1/4 red onion, chopped
1 c. frozen peas
1 c. ranch salad dressing, or more to taste

Cook pasta according to package directions, adding broccoli and carrots during last 3 minutes of cooking time. Drain and rinse with cold water; drain again. Transfer pasta mixture to a large bowl. Add onion and frozen peas; mix well. Stir in one cup salad dressing; cover and chill for 8 hours or overnight. At serving time, stir well; add more salad dressing to taste, if needed. Makes 8 to 10 servings.

You're never too old for party favors! Send your guests home with a whimsical memento...tiny potted plants, little bags of homemade candy, mini photo frames or even jars of bubble solution with wands.

Rainbow Pasta Salad

Sue Haynes
Scottsdale, AZ

This favorite recipe has been in our family for many years! It's delicious...a great recipe for festive occasions. Make it ahead and just pull it from the fridge at serving time.

- 16-oz. pkg. tri-colored rotini pasta, uncooked
- 3 6-oz. jars marinated artichoke hearts, drained
- 2 12-oz. cans black olives, drained
- 15-oz. can garbanzo beans, drained
- 3 to 4 tomatoes, cut into chunks
- 1/4 lb. sliced Genoa salami, cut into quarters
- 3 cloves garlic, finely chopped
- 1/3 c. red wine vinegar
- 1/3 c. olive oil
- 1/4 c. canola oil
- 2 T. dried oregano
- 3/4 c. grated Parmesan cheese

Cook pasta according to package directions; drain. Transfer to a large bowl while still warm. Add all vegetables, salami and garlic; mix gently. Add remaining ingredients except Parmesan cheese; mix well. Add Parmesan and toss lightly. Cover and refrigerate at least 6 hours before serving. Serves 8 to 10.

For the freshest tasting pasta salad, refrigerate some of the prepared dressing separately. Stir the reserved dressing into the salad just before serving. This brightens the color of the salad too.

Casseroles
& Soups
for Sharing

Chicken-Lickin' Croissants with Gravy

Lynda Hart
Bluffdale, UT

These croissants are fancy enough to serve at a luncheon, yet easy enough for a weeknight supper.

4 boneless, skinless chicken breasts, cooked and diced
8-oz. pkg. cream cheese, softened
8-oz. container sour cream
1 c. butter, melted and divided
2 T. onion, grated
1/2 t. garlic, minced
2 8-oz. tubes refrigerated crescent rolls, separated
3/4 c. corn flake cereal, crushed

In a large bowl, mix together chicken, cream cheese, sour cream, 1/2 cup melted butter, onion and garlic. Divide mixture among the 16 crescent triangles, placing near the top of each triangle. Roll up triangles and shape into crescents, tucking in edges. Dip each croissant into remaining butter and then into corn flakes. Arrange on ungreased baking sheets. Bake at 375 degrees for 8 to 12 minutes, until golden. Serve croissants topped with hot Gravy. Makes 8 servings, 2 croissants each.

Gravy:

10-3/4 oz. can cream of chicken soup
1/2 c. whole milk
1 T. lemon juice
1/2 t. lemon pepper

Combine all ingredients in a saucepan over medium-low heat. Cook and stir until smooth and heated through.

Sprigs of fresh herbs in small glasses or bottles make charming table decorations.

Casseroles & Soups *for Sharing*

Inside-Out Ravioli

Janis Parr
Ontario, Canada

This amazing dish is scrumptious and feeds lots of people. If there are any leftovers, they taste even better the next day!

2-1/4 c. elbow macaroni, uncooked
2 T. butter
1 lb. lean ground beef
1/2 c. onion, chopped
1 clove garlic, minced
16-oz. jar spaghetti sauce with mushrooms
8-oz. can tomato sauce
6-oz. can tomato paste
1/2 t. salt
pepper to taste
1-1/4 c. shredded sharp Cheddar cheese
1/2 c. soft bread crumbs
2 eggs, well beaten
1/4 c. oil

Cook macaroni according to package directions; drain. Meanwhile, melt butter in a large skillet over medium heat. Add beef, onion and garlic; cook until beef is browned. Stir in sauces, tomato paste and seasonings; simmer for 10 minutes. In a bowl, combine cooked macaroni, cheese, bread crumbs, eggs and oil. Mix well; spread evenly in a greased 13"x9" baking pan. Spread sauce mixture evenly over top. Bake, uncovered, at 350 degrees for 35 to 40 minutes, until hot and bubbly. Serves 8 to 10.

Warm garlic bread can't be beat! Blend 1/2 cup softened butter and 2 teaspoons minced garlic; spread over a split loaf of Italian bread. Sprinkle with dried parsley. Bake at 350 degrees for 8 minutes, or until hot, then broil briefly, until golden. Cut into generous slices.

Tex-Mex Potato Puff Bake

Cathy Hillier
Salt Lake City, UT

My son and his friends love Mexican food, so this hearty casserole is perfect for them. It's flavorful and easy to make.

1 lb. lean ground beef
1-1/4 oz. pkg. taco seasoning mix
1 c. water
16-oz. jar favorite salsa
2 c. frozen corn
1 c. frozen chopped green pepper & onion blend
16-oz. can pinto beans, drained and rinsed
8-oz. pkg. shredded Mexican-blend cheese, divided
16-oz. pkg. frozen potato puffs
Garnish: sour cream, diced tomatoes, sliced green onions, sliced black olives

Brown beef in a large skillet over medium heat; drain. Stir in seasoning mix, water, salsa and frozen vegetables. Bring to a boil. Reduce heat to low; simmer for 5 minutes, stirring occasionally. Add beans and one cup cheese; mix well and spoon into a greased 13"x9" baking pan. Arrange frozen potato puffs on top. Bake, uncovered, at 400 degrees for 25 minutes, or until bubbly and potato puffs are crisp and golden. Sprinkle with remaining cheese. Return to oven for 5 minutes longer, or until cheese is melted. Garnish with desired toppings. Serves 10.

Keep a big box filled with festive paper napkins and candles... dollar store will do! When surprise guests pop in, you'll be all set to turn an ordinary dinner into a special occasion.

Green Enchilada Casserole

Paula O'Docharty
San Antonio, TX

A family favorite! To spice it up, use shredded Mexican-blend cheese and add 1/4 cup of diced jalapeños. A tasty chopped salad complements this dish.

1 lb. ground beef
1/2 c. onion, diced
7-oz. can diced green chiles
10-3/4 oz. can cream of mushroom soup
1 c. milk
3 c. shredded Cheddar cheese, divided
12 6-inch corn tortillas

Brown beef with onion in a skillet over medium heat; drain. Add remaining ingredients except tortillas, reserving one cup cheese. Layer tortillas and beef mixture in a greased 13"x9" baking pan; top with remaining cheese. Bake, uncovered, at 350 degrees for 30 minutes, or until bubbly and cheese is melted. Serves 8 to 10.

Slow-Cooked Chile Verde

Rita Morgan
Pueblo, CO

So easy and delicious! Ladle it over rice or tortilla chips and add all your favorite toppings.

4-lb. boneless pork shoulder roast, cubed
3 10-oz. cans green enchilada sauce
1 c. salsa verde
4-oz. can chopped green chiles
1/2 t. salt

Combine all ingredients in a 5-quart slow cooker; mix gently. Cover and cook on low setting for 5 to 6 hours, until pork is tender. Makes 10 to 12 servings.

A speedy side for any south-of-the-border dish! Stir salsa and shredded cheese into hot cooked rice. Cover and let stand a few minutes, until cheese melts.

Cheesy Southwest Bean Soup

Tiffany Jones
Batesville, AR

One day I was looking for a soup recipe to feed to my twins, Elizabeth and Noah, and this is what I created. So yummy, and it makes plenty to share. Serve with a basket of crunchy chips.

15-1/2 oz. can black beans, drained and rinsed
15-1/2 oz. can pinto beans, drained and rinsed
15-1/2 oz. can navy beans, drained and rinsed
15-1/2 oz. light red kidney beans, drained and rinsed
15-1/2 oz. can southern-style white beans
15-oz. can white shoepeg corn, drained
14-1/2 oz. can diced tomatoes with green chiles
14-1/2 oz. can diced tomatoes
1-1/4 oz. pkg. taco seasoning mix
1-oz. pkg. ranch seasoning mix
2 c. water
16-oz. pkg. pasteurized process cheese, cubed

In a stockpot, combine all ingredients except cheese; stir. Bring to a boil over medium-high heat. Reduce heat to medium-low and simmer for 25 minutes, stirring often. Add cheese; stir until melted and serve. Serves 10.

A simmering stew or chili is so easy to prepare and always welcomed by guests. Pass a basket of warm bread or tortillas, sit back and enjoy your company!

Easy Taco Soup

Audra Vanhorn-Sorey
Columbia, NC

This is a simple slow-cooker twist on taco soup...and with just six ingredients! Garnish bowls of soup with all your favorite toppings like shredded cheese, sour cream and green onions. Yum!

1 lb. lean ground beef
1-1/4 oz. pkg taco seasoning mix
15-1/2 oz. can kidney beans
15-1/2 oz. can black beans
15-1/4 oz. can corn
14-1/2 oz. can diced tomatoes

Brown beef in a skillet over medium heat; drain and stir in seasoning mix. Transfer beef to a 5-quart slow cooker. Add remaining ingredients; do not drain any of the cans. Stir. Cover and cook on low setting for 4 to 6 hours, stirring occasionally. Makes 8 servings.

Need to feed a few extra guests? It's easy to stretch a pot of soup. Some quick add-ins are canned beans, orzo pasta and instant rice. Add cooked ingredients to the pot and simmer for just a few minutes, until heated through.

Pepperoni Pizza Chili

Cathy Hillier
Salt Lake City, UT

We love to host soup suppers, filling two or three slow cookers with a choice of hot, delicious soups. This one is a favorite. Garlic bread or bread sticks are great go-withs.

- 2 lbs. ground beef
- 1 lb. mild Italian ground pork sausage
- 1 c. onion, chopped
- 1 c. green pepper, chopped
- 4 cloves garlic, minced
- 16-oz. jar favorite salsa
- 15-oz. can pizza sauce
- 1 c. water
- 15-1/2 oz. can hot chili beans
- 15-1/2 oz. can kidney or cannellini beans, drained and rinsed
- 8-oz. pkg. pepperoni slices, halved
- 2 t. chili powder
- 1/2 t. salt
- 1/2 t. pepper
- Garnish: shredded pizza-blend cheese

In a large Dutch oven, combine beef, sausage, onion, green pepper and garlic. Cook over medium heat until beef and sausage are browned; drain. Stir in remaining ingredients except garnish; bring to a boil. Reduce heat to medium-low. Cover and simmer for 20 minutes, or until heated through, stirring occasionally. Top individual servings with cheese. Serves 12.

Bake some savory garlic twists for dinner. Separate refrigerated bread stick dough and lay flat on an ungreased baking sheet. Brush with olive oil; sprinkle with garlic salt and dried parsley. Give each bread stick a twist or two and bake as directed on the package.

Minestrone Soup

Sheila Banks
Albuquerque, NM

This meatless soup is a great recipe to serve in the fall, especially if you can get fresh-picked cabbage at the farmers' market. It is wonderful served with crusty rolls or French bread.

1 c. onion, diced
1/2 c. olive oil
4 c. water
4 cubes beef bouillon
15-1/2 oz. can kidney beans
15-1/2 oz. can Great Northern beans
14-1/2 oz. can diced tomatoes
10-oz. pkg. frozen green beans, thawed
10-oz. pkg. frozen chopped spinach, thawed
4 c. cabbage, chopped
2 potatoes, peeled and diced
2 carrots, peeled and diced
2 zucchini, diced
2 stalks celery, diced

In a large soup pot over medium heat, brown onion in olive oil. Add water, bouillon cubes, undrained beans, undrained tomatoes and remaining ingredients. Bring to a boil; reduce heat to medium-low. Simmer for 2 hours, stirring occasionally, or until vegetables are crisp-tender. Serves 8.

To invite a person into your house is to take charge of his happiness for as long as he is under your roof.

– Anthelme Brillat-Savarin

Creamy Cajun-Spiced Chicken Pasta

Becky Bosen
Syracuse, UT

This is my daughter's favorite recipe whenever she's asked what she wants for dinner. It's super simple to make, but has that "wow" factor! When I serve to guests, they always request the recipe.

16-oz. pkg. linguine or angel hair pasta, uncooked
2 T. olive oil
4 boneless, skinless chicken breasts, cut into strips
4 cloves garlic, minced
1 T. Cajun seasoning blend
1-1/2 c. milk
1/2 c. whipping cream
1/3 c. grated Parmesan cheese

Cook pasta according to package directions; drain. Meanwhile, heat olive oil in a large skillet over medium heat. Add chicken, garlic and Cajun seasoning. Cook until chicken is no longer pink, about 5 minutes, stirring occasionally. Add milk and cream to skillet; stir well. Reduce heat to low. Cook for 5 minutes, or until sauce mixture has thickened. Stir in cheese; cook for 4 to 5 minutes. To serve, ladle chicken and sauce over pasta. Makes 6 to 8 servings.

At sit-down dinners, encourage table talk among guests who don't know each other well. Just write each person's name on both sides of his or her placecard, so other guests can see it.

Casseroles & Soups *for Sharing*

Chicken & Artichoke Casserole

Sandy Wooldridge
Turner, OR

My daughter has become a bit of a foodie...so I was a bit flattered when she asked me for this recipe!

4 boneless, skinless chicken breasts, cut into cubes or strips
14-oz. jar marinated artichoke hearts, drained
8-oz. pkg. crimini mushrooms, sliced
1 c. mayonnaise
1 c. grated Parmesan cheese
1 t. garlic powder
cooked orzo pasta or rice

Arrange chicken in a lightly greased 13"x9" baking pan. Top with artichokes and mushrooms; set aside. In a bowl, mix mayonnaise, Parmesan cheese and garlic powder. Spread mixture over top. Bake, uncovered, at 350 degrees for 30 minutes, or until chicken is no longer pink in the center and juices run clear. To serve, spoon chicken mixture over orzo pasta or rice. Serves 10 to 12.

The flavor of freshly grated Parmesan cheese can't be beat! To keep a chunk of hard cheese fresh, rub softened butter over the cut sides, tuck cheese into a plastic zipping bag and refrigerate.

Colonel Borecky's Chicken

Judy Borecky
Escondido, CA

Here is the recipe for my mother-in-law's drumsticks, which she gave me in the 1960s. She was in a military bridge group and those women had such yummy recipes. We call it Colonel Borecky's Chicken, after my father-in-law. I have also made it with chicken tenders and it's good too. Hope you like it!

1/2 c. low-sodium soy sauce
1/2 c. green olives with pimentos, sliced
1/4 c. sugar
1-1/2 t. ground ginger
1 t. paprika
1 to 2 dashes hot pepper sauce
1 clove garlic, minced
10 chicken drumsticks
10 slices pork or turkey bacon
Garnish: chopped green onions

In a large plastic zipping bag, combine soy sauce, olives, sugar, seasonings, hot sauce and garlic. Add drumsticks to bag. Seal and refrigerate for 2 hours, occasionally turning bag over to coat on all sides. Remove drumsticks from bag; transfer marinade to a small saucepan and bring to a boil. Wrap each drumstick in a slice of bacon; secure with a wooden toothpick and arrange in a greased 13"x9" baking pan. Spoon marinade over drumsticks; cover with aluminum foil. Bake at 350 degrees for 30 minutes; uncover and bake another 30 minutes, or until chicken juices run clear when pierced. Arrange drumsticks on a platter and garnish with onions. Makes 10 servings.

Decorate your dining room table with a sweet table runner. Purchase 2 to 3 yards of cotton fabric in a seasonal print, then edge with rick rack edging and add a tassel at each end. So simple, you'll want to make several!

Sheet Pan Chicken & Peppers

Jen Thomas
Santa Rosa, CA

Oh-so easy! Spoon over steamed rice for an easy and tasty meal.

1/4 c. honey
1 T. soy sauce
1 T. chili sauce
juice of 1 lemon
5 cloves garlic, minced
6 chicken thighs
salt and pepper to taste
1 T. oil
1 green pepper, cubed
1 red pepper, cubed
1 yellow pepper, cubed
1 red onion, sliced

In a bowl, whisk together honey, sauces, lemon juice and garlic. Spoon 1/3 of mixture into a large plastic zipping bag and set aside. Season chicken with salt and pepper; add to bag. Seal bag and turn to coat well; refrigerate at least 30 minutes. Drizzle oil over a 15"x10" jelly-roll pan; transfer chicken to pan and discard bag with sauce. Bake, uncovered, at 400 degrees for 15 to 20 minutes. Remove from oven; arrange vegetables around chicken. Brush chicken with some of the reserved sauce; drizzle remaining sauce over vegetables. Bake another 10 minutes, watching closely, or until chicken is golden and juices run clear. Makes 6 servings.

Dress up the dinner table with some vintage whimsies! Check out local flea markets for salt & pepper shakers in unusual shapes... dancing fruit, hula girls and animals of all shapes and sizes will really spark dinnertime conversations!

Jill's Cheesy Garden Soup

Dara Wills
Hillsboro, OR

I don't care for many vegetables, but when my friend served this soup at book club, I had to try it. Now it's one of my favorite recipes and my family loves it as well. A great way to hide vegetables! This recipe freezes well.

1 c. onion, chopped
1 c. celery, sliced
2 T. butter
2/3 c. all-purpose flour
4 c. water
2 c. frozen broccoli, cauliflower & carrot blend
4 to 6 cubes chicken bouillon
1/4 t. pepper
2 to 3 c. frozen diced potatoes
3 c. milk
2 c. shredded Colby Jack cheese
1 c. shredded Cheddar cheese

In a stockpot over medium heat, cook onion and celery in butter until tender. Stir in flour until smooth. Gradually stir in water; stir in frozen vegetable blend, bouillon cubes and pepper. Bring to a boil. Reduce heat to medium-low; cover and simmer about 8 minutes. Stir in frozen potatoes; continue to simmer another 7 minutes, or until potatoes are tender. Stir in milk and cheeses. Cook and stir over low heat until heated through and cheese melts; do not boil. Serves 10.

Younger guests will feel so grown up when served bubbly sparkling cider or ginger ale in long-stemmed plastic glasses. Decorate with curling ribbon just for fun.

Summer Corn & Potato Chowder

Ann Tober
Biscoe, AR

I love to make this simple soup when there's sweet corn coming out of the garden. Easy to double for more servings.

1/4 c. butter
5 c. fresh corn kernels
2 c. sweet onion, diced
1/2 t. kosher salt
4 c. chicken broth
3 c. potatoes, peeled and diced
3 sprigs fresh thyme, snipped
3/4 c. half-and-half

Melt butter in a stockpot over medium heat; add corn, onion and salt. Cook, stirring occasionally, for 15 to 20 minutes, until corn is tender but not browned. Stir in chicken broth, potatoes and thyme; increase heat to high. Cook, stirring occasionally, for 8 to 10 minutes, until potatoes are tender. Transfer 1/2 cup of soup to a blender; process until smooth and return to stockpot. Stir in half-and-half; serve immediately. Serves 6 to 8.

When cutting the kernels from ears of sweet corn, stand the ear in the center of a tube cake pan. The kernels will fall neatly into the pan.

Carolyn's Goulash

Carolyn Gochenaur
Howe, IN

This is my go-to recipe in wintertime for feeding a big group. Everyone loves it...it never lets me down!

1 c. elbow macaroni, uncooked
3 lbs. ground beef
1/2 to 1 onion, diced
1/2 to 1 green pepper, diced
14-1/2 oz. can petite diced tomatoes
14-1/2 oz. can crushed tomatoes
2 10-3/4 oz. cans tomato soup
15-oz. can tomato sauce
15-1/4 oz. can corn, drained
1/2 c. catsup
2 T. cider vinegar
1 T. sugar
salt and pepper to taste
8-oz. pkg. shredded Cheddar cheese

Cook macaroni according to package directions; drain and set aside. Meanwhile, in a large skillet over medium heat, brown beef with onion and green pepper; drain. Reduce heat to medium-low; simmer for 15 to 20 minutes. Stir in tomatoes with juice and remaining ingredients except cheese. Transfer beef mixture to a greased deep 13"x9" baking pan; add cooked macaroni and mix gently. Sprinkle cheese on top. Bake, uncovered, at 350 degrees for 30 to 40 minutes, until bubbly and heated through. Makes 15 servings.

Before covering a cheese-topped dish with aluminum foil, spray the foil with non-stick vegetable spray. The cheese won't stick to the foil as it melts.

Hearty Potato Soup

Marian Forck
Chamois, MO

Our friends make this tasty soup whenever we all get together on a Saturday night to play cards. It is a big hit! For 12 people you will want to double it...maybe you'll be lucky and have some leftovers.

- 1 c. boiling water
- 5 cubes chicken bouillon
- 7 to 8 baking potatoes, peeled if desired and cubed
- 5 to 6 onions, cubed
- 1 stalk celery, cubed
- 2 c. milk
- 2 8-oz. pkgs. cream cheese, cubed
- salt and pepper to taste
- 1 lb. bacon, crisply cooked and crumbled
- Garnish: chopped green onions, shredded Cheddar cheese

Combine boiling water and bouillon cubes; set aside. Combine potatoes, onions and celery in a soup pot; add enough cold water to cover. Bring to a boil over high heat; reduce heat to medium and simmer until potatoes are tender. Do not drain; add bouillon mixture to soup pot. Stir in milk and cream cheese. Simmer over low heat for 10 to 15 minutes, until blended and cream cheese is melted. Season with salt and pepper. At serving time, stir in bacon. Set out green onions and shredded cheese so everyone can top their own bowls. Makes 6 to 8 servings.

In chilly weather, invite friends to a Soup Supper potluck. Line up slow cookers filled with hearty soups, plus one for hot cider and one for a fruit cobbler. A basket of breads completes the menu...sure to be enjoyed!

Mexican Tortilla Casserole

Tiffany Jones
Batesville, AR

This is a yummy meatless version of a Mexican chicken casserole we like. So delicious!

1 onion, diced
1 green pepper, diced
2 T. olive oil
14-1/2 oz. can diced tomatoes with green chiles
2 10-3/4 oz. cans cream of mushroom soup
16-oz. can pinto beans, drained
15-1/2 oz. can kidney beans, drained
15-1/2 oz. can black beans, drained
1 T. garlic powder
16-oz. pkg. pasteurized process cheese, cubed
6 8-inch flour tortillas, torn into small pieces and divided

In a skillet over medium heat, sauté onion and pepper in oil until tender; drain and set aside. Meanwhile, in a large saucepan over medium heat, combine tomatoes with juice, soup, all beans and garlic powder. Stir well; simmer until well blended. Add cheese; cook and stir until melted. Remove from heat; stir in onion mixture. In a greased 13"x9" baking pan, layer half of tortilla pieces. Top with half of cheese mixture; smooth over tortillas. Layer with remaining tortillas and cheese mixture. Bake, uncovered, at 450 degrees for about 15 minutes, until hot and bubbly. Serves 6 to 8.

Let the kids invite a special friend or two home for dinner. Keep it simple with a hearty casserole and a relish tray of crunchy veggies & dip. A great way to get to know your children's playmates!

Casseroles & Soups
for Sharing

Chicken Dressing Casserole

Judy Wilson
Huntsville, AL

This dish has always been a favorite at our family reunions... we never have any leftovers!

- 8-1/2 oz. pkg. corn muffin mix
- 1/2 c. butter, melted
- 5 boneless, skinless chicken breasts, cooked and diced
- 10-3/4 oz. can cream of celery soup
- 10-3/4 oz. can cream of chicken soup
- 1 c. chicken broth
- 2 eggs, hard-boiled, peeled and chopped

Prepare corn muffin mix and bake in an 8"x8" baking pan, according to package directions. Cool; crumble cornbread into a greased 13"x9" baking pan. Drizzle with melted butter; set aside. In a bowl, mix chicken, soups, broth and eggs. Spoon over cornbread mixture and stir all together. Bake, uncovered, at 325 degrees for 30 to 40 minutes, until heated through. Makes 6 to 8 servings.

Pork Chop & Potato Casserole

Judy Lange
Imperial, PA

A delicious and comforting one-dish dinner. I hope you love it as much as we do!

- 6 pork chops, 1-inch thick
- 1 T. oil
- 1-1/2 t. pepper, divided
- 10-3/4 oz. can cream of celery soup
- 1/2 c. milk
- 1/2 c. sour cream
- 28-oz. pkg. frozen diced potatoes, thawed
- 1 c. shredded Cheddar cheese, divided
- 1 c. French fried onions, divided

In a large skillet over medium heat, brown pork chops in oil. Drain; season with 1/2 teaspoon pepper and set aside. In a bowl, combine soup, milk, sour cream and remaining pepper. Stir in potatoes, 1/2 cup cheese and 1/2 cup onions; spoon mixture into a lightly greased 13"x9" baking pan. Arrange pork chops on top. Cover and bake at 350 degrees for 40 minutes. Uncover; top with remaining cheese and onions. Bake 5 minutes longer, or until cheese melts. Makes 6 servings.

Slow-Cooker Pizza Casserole

Joyceann Dreibelbis
Wooster, OH

A hearty, comforting casserole that the whole family will enjoy.

16-oz. pkg. rigatoni pasta, uncooked
1-1/2 lbs. ground beef
1/2 c. onion, chopped
16-oz. pkg. shredded mozzarella cheese
2 15-oz. cans pizza sauce
10-3/4 oz. cream of mushroom soup
8-oz. pkg. sliced pepperoni

Cook pasta according to package directions; drain. Meanwhile, brown beef with onion in a skillet over medium heat; drain. Place cooked pasta in a 5-quart slow cooker. Stir in beef mixture and remaining ingredients. Cover and cook on low setting for 2 to 3 hours, until bubbly and cheese is melted. Serves 8 to 10.

Tender Roast Pork

Carolyn Gochenaur
Howe, IN

This slow-cooked roast is really delicious and has somewhat of a barbecue flavor to it. Goes well with buttery mashed potatoes.

3-lb. boneless pork roast or tenderloin
8-oz. can tomato sauce
3/4 c. soy sauce
1/2 c. sugar
2 t. dry mustard
Optional: 1 c. cold water, 3 to 4 T. all-purpose flour, salt and pepper to taste

Place roast in a lightly greased 5-quart slow cooker. If necessary, cut roast in half to make it fit. Combine remaining ingredients (except optional ingredients) and pour over roast. Cover and cook on low setting for 8 to 9 hours. Remove roast to a serving platter; cover with aluminum foil and let stand for several minutes before slicing. If gravy is desired, skim fat from crock juices; add to a saucepan over medium heat. Combine water and flour in a jar; cover and shake until well mixed. Slowly add flour mixture to broth. Cook and stir with a whisk until thickened, up to 10 minutes. Season with salt and pepper. Serves 8 to 10.

Baked Veggie Penne Pasta

Hannah Thiry
Luxemburg, WI

A great-tasting dish that everyone enjoys. Just add a salad!

12-oz. pkg. small penne vegetable pasta, uncooked
16-oz. pkg. frozen California-blend vegetables
1 to 2 15-oz jars Alfredo pasta sauce
8-oz. pkg. shredded Italian 6-cheese blend
1/2 c. milk
salt and pepper to taste
1 c. panko-style bread crumbs
2 T. butter, melted

Cook pasta and vegetables separately, according to package directions; drain. In a large bowl, combine cooked pasta, cooked vegetables, Alfredo sauce, cheese and milk. Season with salt and pepper; transfer to a greased deep 13"x9" baking pan. Combine bread crumbs and melted butter; sprinkle over pasta. Bake, uncovered, at 350 degrees for 30 to 35 minutes, until golden. Makes 8 to 10 servings.

A basket brimming with colorful vegetables makes an easy and appealing centerpiece.

Creamy White Chicken Chili

Kimberly Littlefield
Centre, AL

This slow-cooker recipe is a family favorite. We always have a crock full when we invite everyone over to watch football games! For the green chiles, I like to use one can of hot and one can of mild chiles. Set out all the fixin's to top it with...sliced jalapeños and avocados, sour cream, shredded Monterey Jack cheese and crispy tortilla strips.

1 lb. boneless, skinless chicken breasts, fat trimmed
1 t. ground cumin
3/4 t. dried oregano
1/2 t. chili powder
1/4 t. cayenne pepper
1 t. salt
1/2 t. pepper
1 yellow onion, diced
2 cloves garlic, minced
2 15-1/2 oz. cans Great Northern beans, drained and rinsed
2 4-oz cans diced green chiles
15-1/4 oz. can corn, drained
3 c. chicken broth
1 T. fresh cilantro, chopped and loosely packed
1/2 c. reduced-fat cream cheese, softened
1/4 c. half-and-half

Add chicken breasts to a 5-quart slow cooker; sprinkle with seasonings. Top with remaining ingredients except cream cheese and half-and-half; stir. Cover and cook on low setting for 7 to 8 hours, or on high setting for 3 to 4 hours. Remove chicken to a large bowl; let cool, shred and return to mixture in slow cooker. Stir in cream cheese and half-and-half. Cover and cook on high setting for 15 minutes, or until creamy and slightly thickened. Stir well before serving. Makes 8 servings.

Serving finger foods before dinner? Offer small bites like marinated olives that will pique guests' appetites but not fill them up.

Buck-A-Roo-Stew

Faye Mayberry
Benson, AZ

I found this easy chili-like recipe in an old church cookbook. I changed it a bit and spiced it up to give it some great flavor. My family loves it! We like to top it with cheese and enjoy it with tortilla chips.

2 lbs. ground beef
1-1/2 c. onions, diced
28-oz. can crushed tomatoes
15-1/2 oz. can black beans, drained
16-oz. pkg. frozen corn
8-oz. jar medium or hot salsa
2 t. ground cumin
1/2 t. garlic powder

In a large skillet over medium heat, brown beef with onions; drain. Stir in remaining ingredients and bring to a simmer. Reduce heat to medium-low. Simmer for 30 minutes, stirring occasionally. Serves 8 to 10.

It's the unexpected touches that make the biggest impressions. When serving chili or soup, offer guests a variety of fun toppings. Set out bowls with shredded cheese, oyster crackers, chopped onions, sour cream and crunchy croutons, then invite everyone to dig in!

King Ranch Chicken Macaroni & Cheese

Joyce Roebuck
Jacksonville, TX

I have taken this recipe to so many potlucks. Everyone thinks it's wonderful and always ask for the recipe. Try it...I think you will agree!

8-oz. pkg. elbow macaroni, uncooked
2 T. butter
3/4 c. onion, chopped
1 green pepper, diced
10-oz. can diced tomatoes with green chiles
8-oz. pkg. pasteurized process cheese, cubed
3 c. cooked chicken, chopped
10-3/4 oz. can cream of chicken soup
1/2 c. sour cream
1 t. chili powder
1/2 t. ground cumin
1-1/2 c. shredded Cheddar cheese

Cook macaroni according to package directions; drain. Meanwhile, melt butter in a Dutch oven over medium-high heat. Add onion and green pepper; sauté for 5 minutes, or until tender. Stir in tomatoes with juice and cubed cheese. Cook for 2 minutes, stirring constantly, or until cheese melts. Stir in cooked macaroni and remaining ingredients except shredded cheese. Spoon mixture into a lightly greased 13"x9" baking pan. Sprinkle with shredded cheese. Bake, uncovered, at 350 degrees for 25 to 30 minutes, until hot and bubbly. Serves 8 to 10.

Want to try a party-size casserole for your small family? Use two 8"x8" baking pans instead of one 13"x9". Enjoy one dish for dinner tonight, and freeze the other for a future no-fuss meal!

Fast & Easy Chicken Enchiladas

Laura Flood
Markleville, IN

Whenever we want a quick and filling meal or one to share with others, this is a perfect choice! You can make and bake both pans at once, or wrap and freeze one pan to bake later.

5 lbs. boneless, skinless chicken breasts, cooked and shredded
16-oz. container sour cream, divided
16-oz. jar salsa verde, divided
2 10-3/4 oz. cans cream of chicken soup, divided
20 8-inch flour tortillas
16-oz. pkg. shredded mozzarella cheese, divided

In a large bowl, mix together shredded chicken, half of sour cream, half of salsa verde and one can of soup. Fill each tortilla with one tablespoon chicken mixture; sprinkle with one tablespoon shredded cheese and roll up tightly. Arrange 10 filled tortillas in each of 2 greased 13"x9" baking pans. Mix together remaining sour cream, salsa verde and soup; spread evenly over filled tortillas in pans. Sprinkle with remaining shredded cheese. Bake, uncovered, at 375 degrees for 30 minutes, or until cheese is melted and bubbly. Makes 2 pans; each makes 10 servings.

Host an adventure potluck...a terrific way to get together with friends and neighbors. Ask each guest to bring a favorite dish from their hometown, whether that's somewhere across the USA or even around the world. Sure to be tasty and fun!

Tasty Tomato-Basil Soup

Barb Traxler
Mankato, MN

At the peak of tomato season, this recipe makes a tasty luncheon soup. Or ladle it into plastic freezer containers to freeze for a taste of summer in wintertime.

1/4 c. butter
1/2 c. olive oil
4 onions, finely chopped
4 carrots, peeled and finely chopped
4 stalks celery, finely chopped
20 large ripe tomatoes, peeled, seeded and chopped
1 t. sugar
1 c. fresh basil, chopped and divided
salt and pepper to taste
Garnish: sour cream, grated Parmesan cheese

Melt butter with oil in a heavy stockpot over medium heat. Add onions, carrots and celery. Simmer over medium-low heat for about 20 minutes, stirring occasionally, until soft. Add tomatoes, sugar and 3/4 cup basil; simmer for another 20 minutes. Just before serving, add remaining basil; season with salt and pepper. Serve topped with a dollop of sour cream and a sprinkle of Parmesan cheese. Serves 10 to 12.

Peel lots of tomatoes in a jiffy! Cut an "X" in the base of each tomato and place them in a deep saucepan. Add boiling water to cover. After 20 to 30 seconds, remove tomatoes with a slotted spoon and drop them into a sinkful of ice water. The peels will slip right off.

Cream of Broccoli Soup

Lori Rosenberg
Cleveland, OH

From fall to early spring, this soup is a crowd-pleaser!
It's easily doubled too.

1/4 c. plus 1 T. butter, divided
1/4 c. onion, chopped
1/4 c. all-purpose flour
2 c. half-and-half
2 c. chicken broth
1/2 lb. broccoli, chopped
1 c. carrot, peeled and shredded
8-oz. shredded sharp Cheddar cheese
salt and pepper to taste
1/4 t. nutmeg

Melt one tablespoon butter in a small saucepan over medium heat; sauté onion and remove from heat. Meanwhile, melt remaining butter in a large saucepan over medium heat; sprinkle with flour. Cook for 3 to 5 minutes, stirring constantly with a whisk. Stir in half-and-half and chicken broth; simmer over low heat for 20 minutes. Add onion mixture, broccoli and carrot. Cook over low heat for 20 to 25 minutes, stirring occasionally. Add cheese; stir until melted. Stir in seasonings. Serves 4.

Hand-carry a "Special Delivery" greeting to someone who's under the weather and has missed the get-together. Tuck a big jar of comforting soup and a loaf of fresh bread into a basket and tie a ribbon around the handle. Sure to be appreciated!

Easy Oven Barbecue Brisket

Pam Lunn
Pensacola, FL

This delicious brisket cooks all day...the house will smell wonderful. It makes a wonderful buffet dish, and the cold, sliced meat makes scrumptious sandwiches to serve the next day.

4 to 5-lb. beef brisket
smoke-flavored cooking sauce to taste
7 T. butter
1 onion, diced
3/4 c. catsup
1 c. barbecue sauce
1 T. Worcestershire sauce
1 T. red steak sauce
3/4 c. water
1/4 c. brown sugar, packed
2 t. garlic, minced

The night before, pierce brisket all over with a fork; rub with smoke-flavored sauce. Wrap brisket in aluminum foil; place in a baking pan and refrigerate overnight. The next day, remove brisket from refrigerator and let stand at room temperature, 30 to 45 minutes. Do not unwrap. Bake at 400 degrees for 20 minutes. Meanwhile, melt butter in a saucepan over medium heat. Add onion; sauté until tender and golden. Stir in remaining ingredients; simmer for 10 to 15 minutes. Remove brisket from oven; reduce oven temperature to 250 degrees. Open foil and spoon sauce mixture over brisket; reseal in foil. Return brisket to oven. Bake at 250 degrees for 5 to 6 hours, basting occasionally with sauce. Remove from oven. Let brisket stand at room temperature for 10 to 15 minutes; slice against the grain to serve. Serves 8 to 10.

Invite friends and neighbors to a good old-fashioned block party. Set up picnic tables, arrange lots of chairs in the shade and invite everyone to bring a favorite dish. Whether it's a summer cookout or a fall harvest get-together, you'll make some wonderful memories together!

Saucy Pork Ribs

Marcia Shaffer
Conneaut Lake, PA

Who doesn't like pork ribs? Better make plenty, because everyone will want more!

2 lbs. country-style lean pork ribs, cut into serving-size pieces
1 t. seasoned meat tenderizer
14-oz. bottle catsup
1/2 c. onion, grated
1 t. red pepper flakes
salt to taste

Sprinkle ribs with tenderizer. Place in a large stockpot; cover with water. Cover and simmer over medium-low heat for 25 to 30 minutes, until tender. Combine remaining ingredients in a saucepan over medium heat. Bring to a boil; reduce heat to low and simmer for 15 minutes. Drain; arrange ribs in a lightly greased 3-quart casserole dish. Spoon sauce over ribs. Bake, uncovered, at 350 degrees for 30 minutes, or until glazed. Serves 4.

Baked Honey-Garlic Pork Chops

Shirley Howie
Foxboro, MA

These chops are big on flavor and so easy to prepare! Sometimes I use chili sauce instead of catsup. For added zing, try adding a few drops of hot sauce to the glaze.

6 pork chops, 1-inch thick
1/2 c. catsup
2-1/2 T. honey
2 T. low-sodium soy sauce
2 cloves garlic, minced

Place pork chops in a greased 13"x9" baking pan; set aside. In a bowl, whisk together remaining ingredients. Brush glaze over chops. Bake, uncovered, at 350 degrees for 45 minutes, turning chops and brushing with glaze every 15 minutes, until a meat thermometer inserted in the center of chops reads 145 degrees. Makes 6 servings.

Amy's Harvest Chili

Amy Solen
Tennille, GA

My family loves this slow-cooker recipe when the weather starts to change. It warms us right up. Add a basket of cornbread...yum!

1 lb. ground beef
15-1/2 oz. can light red kidney beans
15-1/2 oz. can dark red kidney beans
15-1/2 oz. can Great Northern beans
15-1/2 oz. can pinto beans
15-1/2 oz. can red beans
15-1/2 oz. can chili beans
2 1-1/4 oz. pkgs. mild chili seasoning mix
Garnish: shredded Cheddar cheese, sour cream

Brown beef in a skillet over medium heat; drain. Add all the cans of beans with their juices to a 5-quart slow cooker. Stir in beef and chili seasoning. Cover and cook on low setting for 6 to 8 hours. Garnish as desired. Serves 8.

Simple Chicken Tacos

Amy Theisen
Sauk Rapids, MN

A quick, delicious slow-cooker meal. I like to use black bean salsa.

1-1/2 lbs. boneless, skinless chicken breasts
1-1/4 oz. pkg. taco seasoning mix
16-oz. jar favorite salsa
corn taco shells or tortillas
Garnish: shredded lettuce, chopped tomatoes, shredded Cheddar cheese, sour cream

Place chicken in a 4-quart slow cooker. Sprinkle taco seasoning over chicken; pour salsa on top. Cover and cook on low setting for 6 to 8 hours, or on high setting for 4 hours, until chicken is very tender. Use 2 forks to shred the chicken. Return to slow cooker; stir until mixed well. Serve in taco shells or tortillas with desired toppings. Serves 6 to 8.

Sherry's Chile Egg Puff Casserole

Pat Martin
Riverside, CA

My good friend Sherry always brings this dish to our Bible study potlucks and has given out the recipe to many ladies! I have served it for both brunch and dinner. Since it can be prepared the night ahead, it is a great make-ahead choice for busy occasions. The leftovers (if there are any) are super delicious!

10 eggs, beaten
2 7-oz. cans diced green chiles, drained
16-oz. pkg. shredded Cheddar Jack cheese
16-oz. container cottage cheese
1/2 c. butter, melted
salt and pepper to taste
Optional: favorite salsa

In a large bowl, stir together all ingredients except optional salsa. Spread evenly in a buttered 13"x9" baking pan. Bake, uncovered, at 350 degrees for 35 to 45 minutes, until lightly golden and set. Cool slightly; cut into squares. Serve with salsa, if desired. Makes 10 to 12 servings.

Swap specialties with a friend! For example, offer to trade a kettle of your super-secret-recipe chili for a dozen or two of your best girlfriend's fabulous cupcakes. It's a super way to save dinner-planning time and money.

Andrea's Spicy Hashbrown Quiche

Sandy Perry
Fresno, CA

This delicious recipe can be mixed up a little with different cheeses and meats. The possibilities are endless! Just add a fruit cup and some warm muffins for a wonderful brunch menu.

24-oz. pkg. frozen diced potatoes, thawed and patted dry
1/3 c. butter, melted
1 c. cooked ham, diced
1 c. shredded jalapeño Cheddar cheese
1 c. shredded Monterey Jack cheese
4 eggs, beaten
1/4 t. seasoned salt
1/4 t. pepper
Optional: salsa, sour cream

Press hashbrowns into a lightly greased 9" pie plate to form a crust; brush with melted butter. Bake at 425 degrees for 25 minutes. Meanwhile, combine ham and cheeses in a bowl; spoon evenly into baked crust. In a bowl, whisk together eggs and seasonings; pour into crust. Bake, uncovered, at 425 degrees for 30 to 40 minutes, until center is set when tested with a knife tip. Cut into wedges. Serve with salsa and sour cream, if desired. Makes 8 to 10 servings.

If you like sweet cornbread, you'll love this easy recipe! Mix together an 8-1/2 ounce box of corn muffin mix, a 9-ounce box of yellow cake mix, 1/2 cup water, 1/3 cup milk and 2 beaten eggs. Pour into a greased 13"x9" baking pan and bake at 350 degrees for 15 to 20 minutes. Scrumptious!

Brunch Crescent Casserole

Betty Kozlowski
Newnan, GA

I found a similar recipe online, then made a few changes to make it healthier. The first time I served it, both my grandsons went back for seconds...I think that's a pretty high recommendation!

2 8-oz. tubes refrigerated crescent rolls
1 c. baked turkey ham, cubed
6 green onions, sliced thin
5 eggs, lightly beaten
1 c. milk
1 c. fat-free half-and-half
1 t. salt
1 t. pepper
8-oz. pkg. shredded mozzarella cheese

Separate rolls; roll up each one crescent-style. Arrange rolls in 2 long rows in a greased 13"x9" baking pan. Top with ham and onions; set aside. In a bowl, whisk together remaining ingredients except cheese; fold in cheese and spoon over rolls. Bake, uncovered, at 375 degrees for 20 to 25 minutes, until golden and cheese is melted. Cut into squares. Makes 10 servings.

An apron collection is a whimsical (and practical!) addition to your kitchen. Look for vintage styles at thrift shops and tag sales...hang them from pegs in the kitchen. Everyone can tie on their own ruffled, polka-dotted or flowered favorite whenever they help out in the kitchen.

Fire-Roasted Tomato Gazpacho

Wendy Meadows
Spring Hill, FL

Here in Florida, most of the year it's too hot to enjoy a mug of soup. My grandmother loved tomato soup, so I created a chilled tomato soup that she could enjoy year 'round. The recipe takes just a moment to make and is easily doubled. The longer this chills in the refrigerator, the better the flavor!

14-1/2 oz. can fire-roasted diced tomatoes
1-1/2 c. tomato juice
1 c. cucumber, peeled and chopped
1/4 c. red pepper, finely chopped
2 T. red onion, finely chopped
2 T. fresh cilantro, finely chopped
2 t. white wine vinegar

In a food processor, combine undrained tomatoes and remaining ingredients. Cover; process with quick on-and-off motions until mixture is coarsely puréed. Cover and refrigerate at least one hour before serving, to allow flavors to blend. Serve in chilled bowls. Serves 8.

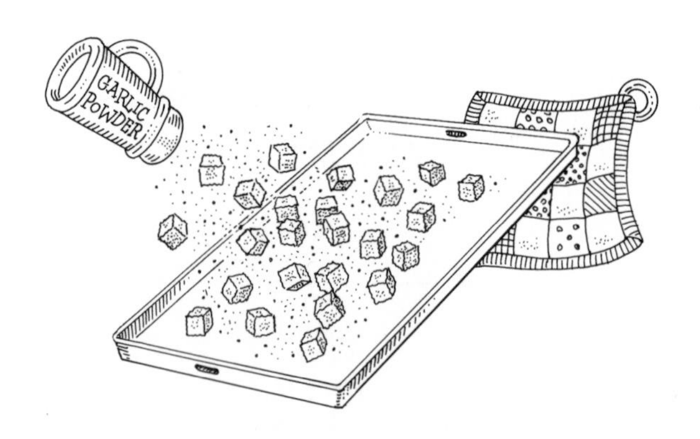

Make the most of leftover slices of country-style bread...turn them into crispy croutons for soups and salads! Toss bread cubes with olive oil and chopped herbs. Toast on a baking sheet at 400 degrees for 5 to 10 minutes, until golden.

Cool-as-a-Cucumber Soup

Gladys Kielar
Whitehouse, OH

Enjoy this soup on a hot summer day. The dill and cucumber make a flavorful, refreshing combination.

1 lb. cucumbers, peeled, seeded and sliced
1/2 t. salt
1-1/2 c. plain yogurt
1 green onion, coarsely chopped
1 clove garlic, minced
4-1/2 t. fresh dill, snipped
Garnish: extra chopped green onion, fresh dill

Place sliced cucumbers in a colander set over a plate; sprinkle with salt and toss. Let stand 30 minutes. Discard liquid, if there is any. Rinse and drain well; pat dry. In a food processor, combine cucumbers, yogurt, onion and garlic; cover and process until smooth. Stir in dill. Immediately ladle into chilled bowls; garnish as desired and serve. Makes 6 servings.

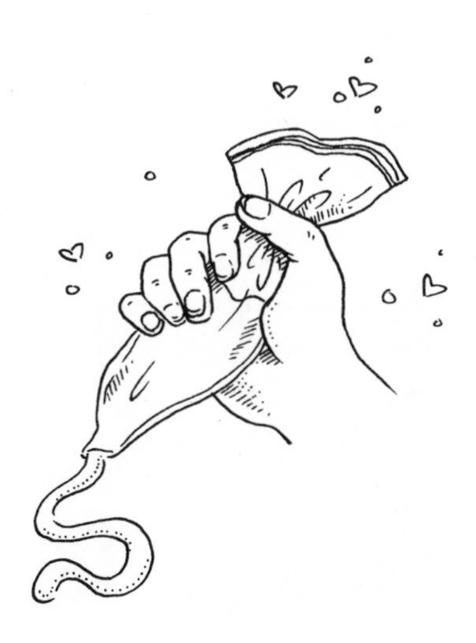

A swirl of sour cream or yogurt dresses up chilled soups in a jiffy. Spoon sour cream into a plastic zipping bag, then seal the bag. Snip a tiny corner from the bag and pipe sour cream in circles over the soup.

Hot Chicken Salad

Diana Krol
Hutchinson, KS

This dish is especially nice to serve at a women's luncheon or take to a salad supper. It's a warm, comforting casserole, not really a salad. I like to serve it with buttered green beans, fruit salad, dinner rolls and a simple dessert.

3-1/2 c. cooked chicken or turkey, cubed
2 10-3/4 oz. cans cream of mushroom soup
1 c. mayonnaise
1-3/4 c. onions, chopped
2-1/4 c. cooked white rice
1-1/2 c. celery, diced
1/2 c. sliced almonds
1-1/2 t. lemon juice
Optional: 1/4 c. sliced pimentos, drained
1 c. shredded Cheddar cheese
1 c. potato chips, crushed

In a large bowl, combine all ingredients except cheese and chips. Mix well; spread evenly in a buttered 13"x9" baking pan. Top with cheese and chips. Bake, uncovered, at 350 degrees for 40 minutes, or until heated through and cheese is melted. Makes 8 to 10 servings.

Serve fizzy juice drinks in glasses with a bit of sparkle. Run a lemon wedge around the rims of glasses, then dip rims in superfine sugar. Garnish each with a sprig of fresh mint.

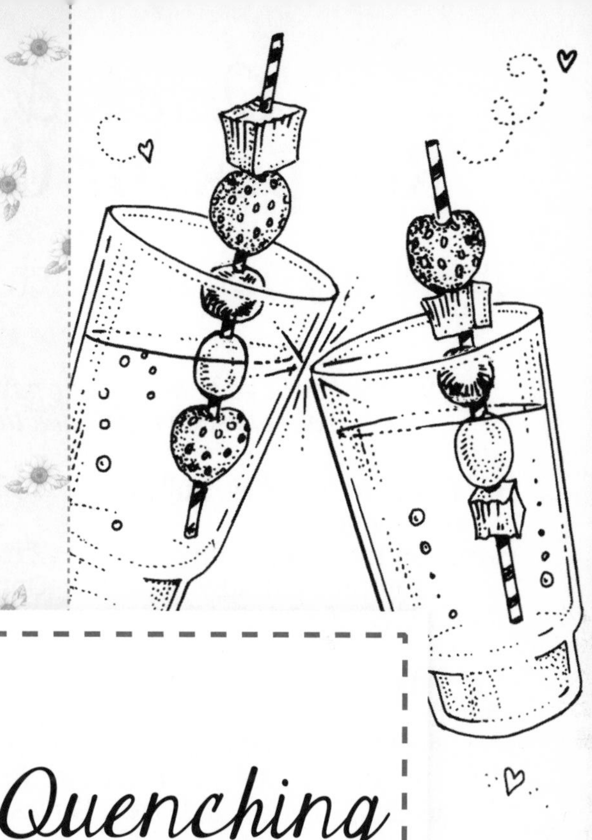

Thirst-Quenching Beverages

Strawberry Daiquiri Punch

Janie Branstetter
Duncan, OK

Just the beverage to make your next gathering extra special. Your guests will feel like they're at a resort!

6 c. fresh strawberries, hulled and divided
6-oz. can frozen limeade concentrate, partially thawed
3/4 c. pineapple juice
16-oz. bottle lemon-lime soda, chilled
2 c. ice cubes
Optional: whole strawberries

Add 3 cups strawberries to a blender or food processor; process until smooth. Transfer blended berries to a large pitcher; repeat with remaining berries. Stir in limeade concentrate and pineapple juice. Cover; chill until serving time. Just before serving, stir in soda and ice. Garnish with additional berries, if desired. Serves 8 to 12.

Peach Lemonade Smoothie

Nancy Kailihiwa
Wheatland, CA

A great summer drink for relaxing outside.

16-oz. pkg. frozen sliced peaches, partially thawed
2 c. prepared lemonade
6-oz. container peach or vanilla yogurt

Combine all ingredients in a blender; process until smooth. Makes 6 servings.

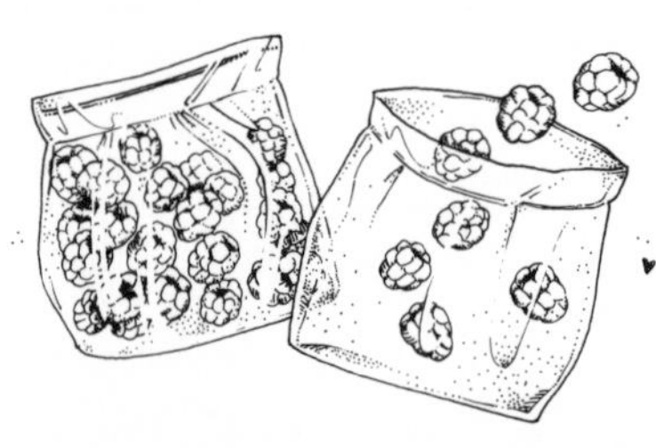

Freeze fresh berries to enjoy year 'round! Spread ripe berries in a single layer on a baking sheet and freeze until solid, then store in plastic freezer bags. Later, pour out just the amount you need.

Thirst-Quenching Beverages

Bahama Breeze

Julie Ann Perkins
Anderson, IN

This is a great get-away drink to take you to "faraway places"... like your backyard!

2-1/2 c. pineapple juice
1 c. strawberries, hulled and sliced
1 ripe banana, sliced
1/2 c. canned coconut cream
2 c. ice cubes
Garnish: fresh pineapple cubes, strawberries and cherries

In a blender, combine all ingredients except garnish. Process until thick and smooth; pour into glasses. Garnish each glass with a skewer of fruit. Makes 6 servings.

Tea-onade

Nancy Johnson
LaVerne, OK

I like iced tea, but I was getting tired of plain iced tea, which I drink unsweetened. So I decided to try adding lemonade mix to it. A young friend came to visit, sampled it and dubbed it Tea-onade.

2 qts. cold water
2 family-size regular or decaf cold-brew tea bags
3/4 c. lemonade drink mix
Optional: 1/8 t. almond extract, 1/8 t. orange extract
ice cubes

Combine cold water and tea bags in a pitcher. Let steep for 3 to 5 minutes, according to strength desired. Stir in lemonade mix until dissolved. Add extracts, if desired. Serve over ice in tall glasses. Makes 8 servings.

Keep it light. Set out a pitcher of chilled sparkling water, dressed up with lemon slices or fresh mint.

Quick & Easy Recipes for Gatherings

Spiced Cranberry Tea

Lynda Robson
Boston, MA

Mom has always served this delicious beverage at Thanksgiving and Christmas...it's a tradition! She serves it in teacups, topped with thin slices of lemon.

1 lb. fresh cranberries
12-1/2 c. water, divided
6 cinnamon sticks
4 whole cloves
zest of 1 orange
12-oz. can frozen orange juice
6-oz. can frozen lemonade
1-1/2 c. sugar

In a large saucepan, combine cranberries, 8 cups water, spices and orange zest. Bring to a boil over medium heat; simmer until cranberries pop. Strain liquid into a large pitcher; discard berries and spices. Add remaining water, frozen concentrates and sugar; stir until sugar dissolves. Serve warm or chilled. Serves 12 to 15.

Festive Punch Cooler

Charlotte Smith
Alexandria, PA

This punch is always a big hit...it's always gone by the end of the evening. Easy and yummy! This makes a green punch... for a peach-colored punch, use orange sherbet.

1 qt. lime sherbet, softened
3 c. pineapple juice, chilled
2 c. orange juice, chilled
2-ltr. bottle lemon-lime soda, chilled

Combine all ingredients in a punch bowl; mix gently. Serve immediately. Makes 20 servings.

Love is the greatest refreshment in life.

– Pablo Picasso

Thirst-Quenching Beverages

Orange Blossom Punch

Gladys Kielar
Whitehouse, OH

I still like using a punch bowl at parties. It reminds me of all the showers and birthday parties our family has had.

3 12-oz. cans frozen orange juice concentrate, thawed
9 c. water
3 12-oz. cans apricot nectar, chilled
3 12-oz. bottles ginger ale, chilled
ice cubes

Combine frozen orange juice and water in a punch bowl; mix well. Add apricot nectar and ginger ale; mix gently. Add ice. Serves 24.

Strawberry Tea Punch

Kathy Courington
Canton, GA

A very good friend made this punch, found in a very old church cookbook with many delicious recipes. It's very refreshing.

6 c. water
1/2 c. instant tea mix
12-oz. can frozen lemonade concentrate
1/2 c. sugar
10-oz. pkg. frozen strawberries, partially thawed
ice cubes

Mix water and tea in a large pitcher; set aside. In a blender, combine frozen lemonade, sugar and strawberries. Process until smooth; combine with tea. Serve over ice. Serves 6 to 8.

For casual parties, a serve-yourself drink dispenser (or 2!) can't be beat.

Fireside Mulled Cider

Vickie
Gooseberry Patch

Fresh ginger and apple jelly are the secret ingredients in this slow-cooker cider! Serve with cinnamon stick stirrers, just for fun.

3 qts. apple cider
1/2 c. apple jelly
1/4 t. nutmeg
2 strips orange peel, 4-inch by 1-inch
3 whole cloves
2 whole allspice
4-inch cinnamon stick
1/2-inch piece fresh ginger, peeled

Combine cider, jelly and nutmeg in a 4-quart slow cooker; set aside. Place remaining ingredients in a square of doubled cheesecloth. Tie with kitchen string and add to slow cooker. Cover and cook on high setting for 4 hours. Discard spice bag before serving. Makes 12 servings.

Spiced Maple Cider

Samantha Starks
Madison, WI

We love sipping on mugs of this delicious cider at our autumn bonfire parties.

2 qts. apple cider
1 c. pure maple syrup
1/3 c. lemon juice
8 whole cloves
1 orange, sliced
3 4-inch cinnamon sticks

Combine cider, syrup and lemon juice in a large saucepan. Insert cloves into one of the orange slices; add all slices and cinnamon sticks to cider mixture. Bring to a boil over medium heat. Reduce heat to medium-low; simmer for 20 minutes. Serve warm. Makes 2 quarts.

Thirst-Quenching Beverages

Hot Cranberry Wassail

Sherry Gordon
Arlington Heights, IL

No holiday gathering is complete without this delicious beverage!

64-oz. bottle cranberry juice cocktail
2-1/2 c. apple juice
Optional: 1/4 c. sugar
3 4-inch cinnamon sticks
1 t. whole allspice
1/2 t. nutmeg
Garnish: whole cloves, orange slices

In a large saucepan over medium heat, combine all ingredients except garnish. Bring to a boil; reduce heat to medium-low and simmer for 10 minutes. Strain punch and discard whole spices. Transfer to a heat-proof punch bowl. Serve in mugs, garnished with clove-studded orange slices. Makes 12 to 15 servings.

Greet visitors with an oh-so-simple harvest decoration that will last from Halloween to Thanksgiving. Roll out an old wheelbarrow and heap it full of large, colorful pumpkins and squash.

Slow-Cooker Pumpkin Spice Latte

Sandra Turner
Fayetteville, NC

I made a double batch of this beverage to share at a church bonfire potluck. It warmed us up on the inside as the bonfire warmed us up on the outside!

7 c. hot brewed coffee
1 c. canned pumpkin
1-1/2 c. half-and-half
1/2 t. nutmeg
1/4 t. cinnamon
1 t. vanilla extract
7 T. sugar
Garnish: whipped cream, nutmeg

Combine all ingredients except garnish in a 5-quart slow cooker; stir. Cover and cook on high setting for 45 minutes to one hour, until hot. Stir again. Serve in mugs, garnished as desired. Serves 8.

Holiday Hot Chocolate

Kathy Grashoff
Fort Wayne, IN

Rich and chocolatey...simple to make.

1-1/2 c. sugar
1/2 c. baking cocoa
1/8 t. salt
5 c. water
12-oz. can evaporated milk
2 c. whole milk
Garnish: whipped cream, crushed peppermints

Combine sugar, cocoa and salt in a large saucepan; stir well. Over high heat, gradually stir in water; bring to a boil. Reduce heat to medium-low. Add milks; heat through but do not boil, stirring occasionally. Pour into mugs; garnish with a dollop of whipped cream and a sprinkle of crushed peppermints. Serves 6 to 8.

A cup of hot cocoa brings out the kid in all of us. Go ahead...treat yourself!

Thirst-Quenching Beverages

Iced Mocha Coffee

Teresa Verell
Roanoke, VA

This recipe is a family favorite. It's a must whenever we're watching movies together on television.

3 c. double-strength brewed coffee, cooled
1 c. whole milk
3 c. chocolate milk
1/2 c. chocolate drink mix
2 to 3 c. crushed ice

Combine all ingredients except crushed ice in a blender. Process well until thoroughly mixed. Divide ice among 4 tall glasses. Pour hot coffee mixture over crushed ice and serve. Serves 4 to 6.

Coffee Ice Cream Punch

Connie Bryant
Topeka, KS

A refreshing beverage for summer get-togethers.

1 gal. strong brewed coffee, cooled
2 qts. coffee ice cream, divided
1 pt. vanilla ice cream
Garnish: whipped cream, chocolate sprinkles

In a punch bowl, combine coffee and one quart coffee ice cream; mix to a fairly thick consistency. Cover and refrigerate until chilled. At serving time, scoop vanilla ice cream and remaining coffee ice cream into balls; add gently to punch bowl. Serve in mugs; top generously with whipped cream and sprinkles. Serves 20 to 30.

Just for fun, set out snowman-shaped candy marshmallows to float in hot cocoa.

Not Your Everyday Punch

Jill Williams
Riley, KS

This punch is a family favorite and has been served at many special family occasions...weddings, showers and anniversaries. Just choose the color of the gelatin mix to match your occasion. It's also a great summertime treat to keep in your freezer.

13 c. water, divided
3 3-oz. pkgs. favorite-flavor gelatin mix
4 c. sugar
3 c. lemon juice
2 46-oz. cans pineapple juice, chilled
4 qts. ginger ale, chilled if desired

Bring 9 cups water to a boil in a stockpot over high heat. Add gelatin mix; stir until dissolved and remove from heat. In a saucepan, bring remaining 4 cups water to a boil. Add sugar and stir until dissolved; add to gelatin mixture. Allow to cool. Stir in lemon and pineapple juices. Pour punch into plastic freezer containers; cover and freeze for at least 24 hours. One hour before serving, remove frozen punch from freezer. Break up punch and add to a punch bowl; gently pour in ginger ale. Serves 64.

Note: Using room-temperature ginger ale will make this more of a punch; for a slush-type drink, use chilled ginger ale.

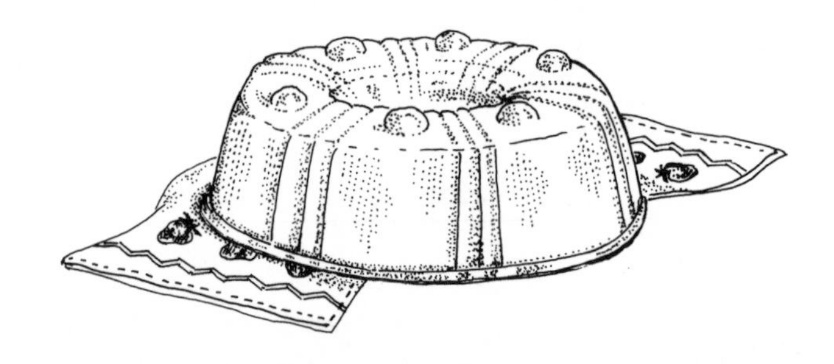

For a beautiful fruit-studded ice ring, arrange berries, sliced oranges, lemons and limes in a ring mold. Pour in a small amount of punch; let freeze. Repeat until mold is filled and turn out of mold.

Thirst-Quenching Beverages

Ginger Lemonade

Ellie Brandel
Milwaukie, OR

Ginger adds a different tang to lemonade! Freeze some of this into ice cubes to use in the drinks, so they won't be diluted.

1-1/2 c. sugar
2 qts. water
7 thin slices fresh ginger root, peeled
2 c. lemon juice
ice cubes
Garnish: lemon slices

In a large saucepan, combine sugar, water and ginger. Bring to a boil over high heat, stirring occasionally. Remove from heat; stir in lemon juice and cool for 15 minutes. Discard ginger. Chill at least one hour. Serve over ice, garnished with lemon slices. Serves 10.

Perfectly Pink Lemonade

Jill Ball
Highland, UT

There is something so satisfying about sitting in the summertime sipping on a tall icy glass of pink lemonade. For some reason, lemonade just tastes better when it's pink!

6 c. cold water
1 c. lemon juice
1 c. sugar
several drops red food coloring
ice cubes

Combine all ingredients except ice in a pitcher; stir until sugar dissolves. Chill; serve over ice. Makes 8 servings.

Fill a big glass jar with vintage-style candies...guests of all ages will love scooping out their favorites!

Watermelon Limeade

JoAnn
Gooseberry Patch

Sweet, tangy, frosty...a super thirst quencher!

3 c. watermelon, cubed and seeded
4 c. water
1/4 c. sugar
1/4 c. lime juice
crushed ice
Garnish: fresh mint sprigs or mini watermelon wedges

Add watermelon cubes to a blender; process until smooth and add to a pitcher. Stir in water, sugar and lime juice; chill. Serve over crushed ice, garnished with sprigs of fresh mint or skewers of watermelon. Makes 6 servings.

Lemony Cooler

Tiffany Brinkley
Broomfield, CO

So refreshing! I like to freeze some of it in ice cube trays to add to the glasses...add lemon twists to the cubes, just for fun.

3 c. white grape juice
1/2 c. lemon juice
1/2 c. sugar
1-ltr. bottle club soda, chilled
ice cubes

In a pitcher, combine grape juice, lemon juice and sugar; stir until sugar dissolves. Chill. Add club soda at serving time; serve over ice. Serves 8.

Serving outdoors? Keep pesky insects away from beverage pitchers. Stitch 4 large beads to the corners of a table napkin and drape over the open pitcher.

Thirst-Quenching Beverages

Lemonade Iced Tea

Jennie Gist
Gooseberry Patch

When I was growing up, my aunt always served a similar beverage at family gatherings. Hers tasted memorably different, since the water at her home in the country came from a well.

3 c. boiling water
4 tea bags
12-oz. can frozen lemonade concentrate, thawed
2 c. cold water
ice cubes
Garnish: thin lemon slices

In a large pitcher, combine boiling water and tea bags; let stand for 10 minutes. Discard tea bags. Add lemonade concentrate and cold water; stir to blend. Chill. Serve over ice, garnished with lemon slices. Makes 8 servings.

Southern Sweet Tea

Staci Prickett
Montezuma, GA

I love my sweet tea, and this is the best way to make it! And a couple of tips: use warm water from the faucet, never heated. If you make a batch of sweet tea that turns out bitter, just sprinkle a pinch of baking soda in the pitcher and stir...bitterness is gone.

1 gal. warm water
2 family-size tea bags
1-1/2 to 2 c. sugar
ice cubes

Fill a one-gallon pitcher with warm water; add tea bags. Steep for 8 hours or overnight. Remove tea bags; do not squeeze. Stir in sugar to taste; serve over ice. Makes 16 servings.

For crystal-clear ice cubes, bring a tea kettle of tap water to a boil. Cool to room temperature and pour into ice cube trays.

Raspberry Sherbet Punch

Janice Schuler
Alburtis, PA

Whenever I make this punch, I remember Mom making it for my baby shower. It always brings back wonderful memories! I make this in the summer for bridal and baby showers or going-away parties at work. Great for luncheons and parties with just finger foods too!

2 c. boiling water
1/2 c. sugar
1 c. fresh mint, or 1/4 c. dried mint
2 10-oz. pkgs. frozen red raspberries
12-oz. can frozen pink lemonade concentrate
5 c. cold water
2 qts. raspberry sherbet

In a large bowl, combine boiling water, sugar and mint; let stand 5 minutes. Add raspberries and lemonade concentrate; stir until thawed. Using a fine mesh strainer or cheesecloth, strain mixture, discarding berries. Pour liquid into a large pitcher; add cold water and chill overnight. At serving time, transfer punch to a punch bowl; float scoops of sherbet on top. Makes 30 servings.

A large clear glass punch bowl is a must for entertaining family & friends. Serve up a frosty punch, a sweet dessert trifle or even a layered salad... you'll wonder what you ever did without it!

Special Occasion Desserts

Aunt Ginger's Famous Coffee Cake

Ginger Mason
Seward, NE

This recipe is so special because it is delicious. My daughters, nieces & nephews and others just love it. It is an easy recipe and the sour cream makes it nice and moist. Very good!

2-1/2 c. all-purpose flour
1 c. sugar
1 c. brown sugar, packed
1 c. corn oil
1/2 t. cinnamon
1/2 t. salt
8-oz. container sour cream
2 eggs, beaten
1 t. vanilla extract
1 t. baking powder
1 t. baking soda
Optional: 1/2 c. chopped nuts

In a large bowl, mix together flour, sugars, oil, cinnamon and salt; set aside one cup of mixture in another large bowl. To remaining flour mixture, add sour cream, eggs, vanilla, baking powder and baking soda; mix well. Stir in nuts, if using. Pour batter into a greased 13"x9" baking pan. Sprinkle reserved flour mixture over top. Bake at 350 degrees for 30 to 45 minutes. Cut into squares. Makes 15 servings.

Simple touches make a gathering special! At dessert time, set out whipped cream and shakers of cinnamon and cocoa for coffee drinkers. Tea drinkers will love a basket of special teas with honey and lemon slices.

Apricot & Ice Cream Dessert Torte

Marcia Marcoux
Charlton, MA

A delectable dessert that's easily made in advance.
It's a favorite for warm days!

1 c. vanilla wafers, finely crushed
1/2 c. almonds, coarsely chopped and toasted
1/4 c. butter, melted
1/2 t. almond extract
3 pts. vanilla ice cream, softened and divided
1 c. apricot preserves, divided
Optional: whipped cream

In a bowl, combine vanilla wafer crumbs, almonds, melted butter and extract; toss to mix. Sprinkle 1/3 of crumbs evenly in a buttered, aluminum foil-lined 8"x8" baking pan. Spoon half of ice cream over crumbs. Spread 1/2 cup preserves over ice cream; sprinkle with half of remaining crumbs. Cover with remaining ice cream and preserves; sprinkle with remaining crumbs. Cover and freeze until firm. Cut into squares; top with a dollop of whipped cream, if desired. Makes 9 servings.

Use a food processor or blender to quickly crush cookies for crumb crusts. If you don't have one handy, place cookies in a large plastic zipping bag and crush them with a rolling pin.

Helen's Lemon Bars

Carol Gray
Peoria, AZ

I am a snowbird here in Arizona and got this recipe from my neighbor Helen, who makes the best lemon bars. Everyone loves them! We have a lot of lemon trees in our neighborhood and this is a great way to enjoy using the lemon juice.

2-1/4 c. all-purpose flour, divided
1/2 c. powdered sugar
1 c. butter
4 eggs
2 c. sugar
1/3 c. lemon juice
1/2 t. baking powder
Garnish: additional powdered sugar

In a bowl, sift together 2 cups flour and powdered sugar. Cut in butter until mixture clings together. Press into the bottom of a lightly greased 11"x9" baking pan. Bake at 350 degrees for 20 to 25 minutes; set aside. Beat eggs in another bowl; beat in sugar and lemon juice. Stir in remaining flour and baking powder; pour over baked crust. Return to oven for 25 minutes. Remove from oven; sprinkle with additional powdered sugar. Cool. Cut into 2-inch bars. Makes 20 bars.

Turn mismatched teacups upside-down and set a pretty saucer on top to give each guest their own individual cake stand. A fun way to serve cookie bars and cupcakes!

Special-Occasion Desserts

Brown Sugar Squares

Delores Lakes
Mansfield, OH

This is a tasty and quick dessert to enjoy with ice cream and coffee, or just by itself. If a friend were to call me and say she wanted to come to my house in an hour, I could whip these up in a jiffy and serve them fresh out of the oven!

1 unbeaten egg
1 c. brown sugar, packed
1 t. vanilla extract
1/2 c. all-purpose flour
1/4 t. baking soda
1/4 t. salt
1 c. coarsely chopped walnuts

In a bowl, stir together egg, brown sugar and vanilla. Quickly stir in flour, baking soda and salt; fold in walnuts. Spread batter in a greased 8"x8" baking pan. Bake at 350 degrees for 18 to 20 minutes; will be soft in center. Cool in pan on a wire rack; cut into squares. Makes one dozen.

Famous Gooey Butter Cake

Patti Cunningham
Saint Louis, MO

Here in Saint Louis, we claim we invented this yummy cake!

18-1/4 oz. pkg. butter recipe cake mix
1/2 c. butter, melted
2 eggs, divided
8-oz. pkg. cream cheese, softened
16-oz. pkg. powdered sugar

In a large bowl, beat together dry cake mix, melted butter and one egg. Pour batter into a greased 13"x9" baking pan. In another bowl, blend cream cheese, powdered sugar and remaining egg; spoon over batter. Bake at 350 degrees for 40 to 45 minutes; center will be gooey. Cool; cut into squares. Makes one dozen.

No matter where I serve my guests,
they seem to like my kitchen best.
– Old Saying

Strawberry Delight

Karen Gierhart
Fremont, OH

This luscious dessert is often requested for family parties. It's easy to make and only uses a few ingredients. It may be made a day or two ahead...just pull from the fridge at dessert time.

1 angel food cake, broken into small pieces
3-oz. pkg. instant vanilla pudding mix
1 c. milk
1 pt. vanilla ice cream, softened
3-oz. pkg. strawberry gelatin mix
1 c. boiling water
16-oz. pkg. container frozen strawberries, partially thawed
8-oz. container frozen whipped topping, thawed

Spread cake pieces evenly in an ungreased 13"x9" glass baking pan; set aside. In a bowl, combine pudding mix and milk; whisk for 2 minutes. Add ice cream and stir. Spoon pudding mixture over cake and work down through cake pieces. Cover and refrigerate for 15 minutes. In another bowl, combine gelatin mix and boiling water; stir for 2 minutes, or until dissolved. Add strawberries; stir until thawed and gelatin starts to thicken. Spoon over cake mixture. Cover and refrigerate for several hours. At serving time, spread with whipped topping. Serves 12.

Offer mini portions of rich cobblers, cakes or pies in small Mason jars...how charming!

Blueberry Cheesecake Punch Bowl Trifle

Tiffany Jones
Batesville, AR

This dessert looks as pretty as it tastes! I came up with this last-minute recipe for a wedding shower at work...it was a huge hit!

1 angel food cake, cubed
2 8-oz. pkgs. cream cheese, room temperature
3/4 c. whipping cream
1/2 c. sour cream
1 t. vanilla extract
1 c. powdered sugar
21-oz. can blueberry pie filling, divided

Add cake cubes to a punch bowl; set aside. In another bowl, combine remaining ingredients except pie filling; beat with an electric mixer on medium speed until smooth and creamy. Spoon half of cream cheese mixture over cake; dollop with half of pie filling. Repeat layers. Cover and chill until serving time. Makes 10 servings.

Create a fun centerpiece for an ice cream social. Clean an empty ice cream container (or ask the local store for extras), fill with floral foam and tuck in some bright flowers.

Triple Chocolate Bundt Cake

Tamela James
Grove City, OH

This is a really moist, delicious, easy cake to make. I have made this for years and am always asked for the recipe.

- 18-1/4 oz. pkg. devil's food or dark chocolate fudge cake mix
- 3.9-oz. pkg. instant chocolate pudding mix
- 8-oz. container sour cream
- 1/2 c. water
- 1/2 c. oil
- 4 eggs, beaten
- 1-1/2 c. semi-sweet chocolate chips
- Garnish: favorite chocolate frosting

In a large bowl, combine dry cake and pudding mixes, sour cream, water, oil and eggs in a large bowl; mix thoroughly. Fold in chocolate chips. Pour batter into an oiled and floured 12-cup Bundt® pan. Bake at 350 degrees for 58 to 62 minutes, until cake is just starting to pull away from the sides and springs back when lightly pressed with a finger. Cool in pan on a wire rack for 20 minutes. Invert cake onto rack and cool completely. Spread with frosting as desired. Serves 12 to 15.

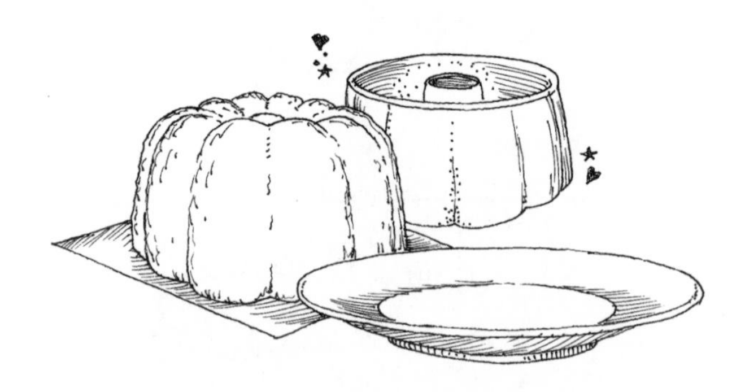

Easily turn a Bundt® cake out of its pan. Just before it is finished baking, lay a folded bath towel in the sink and soak with very hot water. Remove the cake from the oven and immediately set it on the towel, pan-side down, for 10 seconds. Invert the pan onto a cake plate and cool completely.

Apple-Walnut Cake

Toni Groves
Benld, IL

I got this scrumptious recipe from a co-worker... my family loves it!

4 c. Granny Smith apples, peeled, cored and coarsely chopped
1 c. black walnuts, chopped
2 c. sugar
2 c. all-purpose flour
2 t. baking soda
1/2 t. salt
2 t. cinnamon
2 eggs
1/2 c. oil
2 t. vanilla extract
Garnish: whipped cream

In a large bowl, combine apples, walnuts and sugar; toss to mix well and let stand for 20 minutes. In another bowl, sift together flour, baking soda, salt and cinnamon; set aside. In another large bowl, beat eggs, oil and vanilla. Alternately add flour mixture and apple mixture to egg mixture; stir well after each addition. Pour batter into a generously greased and floured Bundt® pan. Bake at 350 degrees for one hour, or until a toothpick inserted near the center comes out clean. Cool in pan; turn cake out onto a cake plate. Serve chilled with whipped cream. Makes 12 to 15 servings.

Jazz up homemade apple desserts in a jiffy. Top with a drizzle of warm caramel sauce...scrumptious!

Pecan Pie Squares

Elaine Divis
Sioux City, IA

This is a favorite at church potlucks, family gatherings and especially at the holidays. It's an easy and tasty way to serve pecan pie to a crowd. My pan always comes home empty!

3 c. all-purpose flour
1-1/2 c. plus 6 T. sugar, divided
3/4 c. butter, softened
3/4 t. salt
4 eggs, lightly beaten
1-1/2 c. light corn syrup
3 T. butter, melted
2 t. vanilla extract
2-1/2 c. chopped pecans

In a bowl, combine flour, 6 tablespoons sugar, softened butter and salt. Beat with an electric mixer on low speed until crumbly; mixture will be dry. Press firmly into a greased 15"x10" jelly-roll pan. Bake at 350 degrees for about 20 minutes, until lightly golden. Meanwhile, in another bowl, mix together eggs, remaining flour, corn syrup, melted butter and vanilla; stir in pecans. Pour filling into baked crust; spread evenly. Bake at 350 degrees for about 25 minutes, until filling is set. Cool. Cut into squares. Makes 3 dozen.

Chocolaty S'mores Bars

Kelly Alderson
Erie, PA

These bars are really irresistible...almost as good as making s'mores over a campfire!

1/4 c. butter, cubed
10-oz. pkg. marshmallows
12-oz. pkg. bite-size graham cereal squares
1/3 c. milk chocolate chips, melted

In a large saucepan, melt butter over low heat. Add marshmallows; cook and stir until melted and well blended. Remove from heat. Stir in cereal until coated. Press into a greased 13"x9" baking pan using a buttered spatula. Drizzle with melted chocolate. Cool completely; cut into squares. Store in an airtight container. Makes 1-1/2 dozen.

Pat's Cookies & Cream Ice Cream Squares

Pat Beach
Fisherville, KY

This is the easiest and best frozen dessert you will ever taste. I have been making this super-easy and absolutely delicious dessert for my family for over 35 years. I made it quite often for my daughters as they were growing up, and am now spoiling my grandchildren with this delicious dessert. It is always a big hit and everyone is so surprised at how easy it is to prepare.

1-1/2 qts. vanilla ice cream
8-oz. container frozen whipped topping, thawed
18-oz. pkg. chocolate sandwich cookies, crushed

Place ice cream in a large bowl; let stand at room temperature until softened. Stir the softened ice cream until smooth; fold in whipped topping until thoroughly combined. Fold crushed cookies into ice cream mixture; spoon into an ungreased 13"x9" baking pan. Cover and freeze until frozen. Set out about 10 minutes before serving. Cut into squares and serve. Makes 12 to 15 servings.

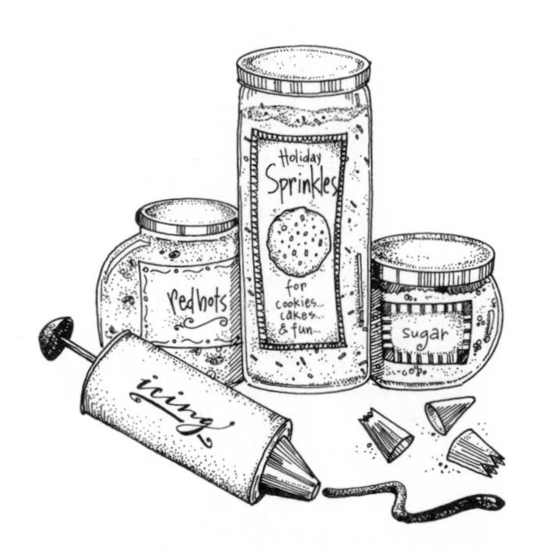

A toss of candy sprinkles makes any dessert special! Check out the baking department at your neighborhood craft store for a wide selection of mini candies and colorful sprinkles to dress up desserts in a jiffy.

Frozen Peach Cream Pie

Charlotte Smith
Alexandria, PA

This is an easy, quick recipe. It's a refreshing cool dessert on a hot summer day. Frozen, thawed peaches may be used as well. This makes 2 pies...plenty to share with friends!

1-1/2 c. peaches, peeled, pitted and sliced
8-oz. pkg. cream cheese, softened
14-oz. can sweetened condensed milk
1 T. lemon juice
8-oz. container frozen whipped topping, thawed
2 9-inch graham cracker crusts
Optional: additional peach slices

Purée peaches in a food processor or blender; set aside. In a large bowl, beat cream cheese with an electric mixer on medium speed until fluffy. Gradually beat in condensed milk; stir in puréed peaches and lemon juice. Fold in whipped topping. Divide peach mixture evenly between crusts. Cover and freeze for 4 hours, or until firm. At serving time, let stand at room temperature for a few minutes; cut into wedges. Garnish with additional peach slices, if desired. Makes 2 pies; each serves 8.

Take-out boxes are available in lots of festive colors and patterns. Keep some handy for wrapping up food gifts in a jiffy...and for sending home dessert with guests who just can't eat another bite!

Special-Occasion Desserts

Berry Dessert Topping

Charity Miller
Tustin, MI

This is one of my favorite recipes for topping cheesecakes... it would also be good spooned over ice cream. I like to use a frozen triple-berry mix, but it's yummy with just one kind of berry too.

- 6 c. frozen blackberries, blueberries, raspberries and/or strawberries, partially thawed and divided
- 1 c. sugar
- 3 T. cornstarch
- 1/2 c. water

Mash one cup berries in a large saucepan; set aside. Mix together sugar and cornstarch in a small bowl. Add sugar mixture and water to mashed berries; stir until combined. Cook and stir over medium heat until mixture boils and thickens. Boil one minute longer; remove from heat. Cool to lukewarm; stir in remaining whole berries. Cool completely before serving. Makes 6 servings.

Instant ice cream social! Alongside pints of ice cream, set out toppings like sliced bananas, peanuts, hot fudge sauce and whipped cream. Don't forget the cherries!

Pineapple Sheet Cake

Ramona Storm
Gardner, IL

A simple cake to put together. Serve it from the pan for casual entertaining, or cut and arrange it on a cake plate for something a little more special.

2 c. all-purpose flour
2 c. sugar
2 eggs, beaten
1 c. chopped nuts, divided
2 t. baking soda
1/2 t. salt
1 t. vanilla extract
20-oz. can crushed pineapple

In a large bowl, combine flour, sugar, eggs, 3/4 cup nuts, baking soda, salt and vanilla. Stir in pineapple with juice until well blended. Pour batter into a greased 15"x10" jelly-roll pan. Bake at 350 degrees for 20 to 22 minutes, until a toothpick inserted in the center comes out clean. Cool in pan on a wire rack. Spread cake with Icing; sprinkle with remaining nuts. Makes 24 servings.

Icing:

8-oz. pkg. cream cheese, softened
1/2 c. butter, softened
3-1/2 c. powdered sugar
1 t. vanilla extract

In a large bowl, beat together all ingredients until smooth and spreadable.

Taking a cake to a potluck or get-together? Before covering in plastic wrap, insert toothpicks into the cake and top with mini marshmallows. They'll keep the plastic wrap from touching the frosting.

Coconut Cream Ice Cream Dessert

Deborah Kraus
Pittsburgh, PA

This dessert is a big hit at our family gatherings every time. Everyone always asks for the recipe!

2 sleeves round buttery crackers, crushed
1/2 c. butter, melted
1/2 gal. vanilla ice cream, softened
1 c. milk
2 3.4-oz. pkgs. instant coconut cream pudding mix
8-oz. container frozen whipped topping, thawed
1 c. shredded coconut

In a bowl, mix together crushed crackers and melted butter. Spread evenly in the bottom of a lightly greased 13"x9" baking pan; set aside. In another bowl, blend together ice cream, milk and dry pudding mix; spread over cracker mixture. Top with whipped topping; sprinkle with coconut. Cover and freeze overnight. Cut into squares. Makes 12 to 16 servings.

Make a good thing even better...sprinkle ice cream desserts with toasted coconut. Spread shredded coconut on an ungreased baking sheet. Bake at 350 degrees for 7 to 12 minutes, stirring often, until toasted and golden. Cool before using.

Chocolate Zucchini Sheet Cake

Mary Patenaude
Griswold, CT

This is a great dessert for summer picnics and other get-togethers. Not only is it delicious, it travels well and the frosting doesn't get sticky.

2 c. sugar
1 c. oil
3 eggs, beaten
2-1/2 c. all-purpose flour
1/4 c. baking cocoa
1/4 t. baking powder
1 t. baking soda
1/4 t. salt
1/2 c. milk
2 c. zucchini, shredded
1 T. vanilla extract

In a large bowl, stir together sugar and oil. Add eggs; beat well and set aside. In another bowl, combine flour, cocoa, baking powder, baking soda and salt. Gradually add flour mixture to egg mixture alternately with milk; mix well. Stir in zucchini and vanilla. Pour batter into a greased 15"x10" jelly-roll pan. Bake at 375 degrees for 25 minutes, or until cake tests done with a toothpick. Spread Frosting over cake while still hot. Cool in pan on a wire rack. Cut into squares. Serves 20.

Frosting:

1/2 c. butter, softened
1/4 c. baking cocoa
6 T. evaporated milk
4 c. powdered sugar
1 T. vanilla extract

Combine all ingredients in a large bowl; beat until smooth.

Sheet cakes are party-perfect! A cake baked in a jelly-roll pan will yield as many as 35 pieces, if cut into 2-inch squares. Between slices, simply dip the cake knife in hot water and wipe it clean with a paper towel.

Berry Patch Slab Pie

Kelly Alderson
Erie, PA

Is there a better way to treat lots of guests to summer-ripe berries? I don't think so! Mix it up...add some raspberries and blackberries too, and a big dollop of whipped cream.

14.1-inch pkg. refrigerated pie crusts
2 8-oz. pkgs. cream cheese, softened
2/3 c. sugar
1 T. milk
3 c. strawberries, hulled and sliced
3 c. blueberries
1 c. strawberry glaze

Soften pie crusts as directed on package. On a lightly floured surface, unroll crusts and stack one on top of the other. Roll out to a 17-inch by 12-inch rectangle. Fit doubled crust into an ungreased 15"x10" jelly-roll pan, pressing crust into corners of pan. Crimp edges of crust; pierce crust all over with a fork. Bake at 350 degrees for 10 to 12 minutes, until golden. Set on a wire rack to cool completely, about 30 minutes. In a bowl, blend cream cheese, sugar and milk until smooth. Spread mixture onto cooled crust with a spatula. Chill for about one hour, until set. In a large bowl, combine all berries and glaze; mix gently. Spoon berry mixture over cream cheese. Cover and refrigerate until serving time. Cut into squares. Makes 24 servings.

Scoop ice cream into a muffin tin and freeze. At dessert time, each scoop will be all ready for serving up cake & ice cream or pie à la mode...no muss, no fuss!

Pumpkin Crown Cake

Sandy Coffey
Cincinnati, OH

This cake is so good for a luncheon dessert over coffee or tea, for guests at home or church functions. The sauce is heavenly on the cake, and could also be used on other cakes of choice.

18-1/2 oz. pkg. yellow cake mix
3.4-oz. pkg. instant butterscotch pudding mix
4 eggs, beaten
1/4 c. water
1/4 c. oil
1 c. canned pumpkin
2 t. pumpkin pie spice
Optional: powdered sugar

In a large bowl, combine all ingredients except optional powdered sugar. Beat with an electric mixer on low speed until mixed; continue beating on medium-high speed for 4 minutes. Pour batter into a greased and floured 10" Bundt® or tube pan. Bake at 350 degrees for 50 to 55 minutes. Cool in pan for 15 minutes. Turn cake out of pan; finish cooling on a wire rack. Serve topped with Creamy Vanilla Sauce or powdered sugar. Makes 8 to 10 servings.

Creamy Vanilla Sauce:

3.4-oz. pkg. instant vanilla pudding mix
2 c. light cream or half-and-half

Combine pudding mix and cream or half-and-half in a large bowl. Beat with an electric mixer on low speed until blended. Beat on medium-high speed 2 more minutes; let stand for 5 minutes. Cover and refrigerate. Just before serving, stir until creamy.

Fill a vintage-style shaker with powdered sugar...so handy for sprinkling on cakes, cookies and even breakfast waffles!

Apple-Pecan Dump Cake

Mel Chencharick
Julian, PA

This recipe is so simple and so good. Serve warm, topped with vanilla ice cream and drizzled with caramel ice cream topping. Yummy! This cake is great any time.

2 21-oz. cans apple pie filling
1 t. apple pie spice or cinnamon
1/2 t. nutmeg
1/2 t. allspice
18-1/4 oz. pkg. butter pecan cake mix
3/4 c. butter, thinly sliced
1/2 c. chopped pecans

Spread pie filling in a buttered 13"x9" baking pan. Combine spices in a cup; sprinkle over pie filling. Sprinkle dry cake mix over all. Arrange butter slices all over the surface; sprinkle with pecans. Bake at 350 degrees for 45 minutes to one hour, until bubbly and golden on top. Cut into squares; serve warm. Makes 12 servings.

If dessert is a flop, layer it with whipped cream in a parfait glass and give it a fancy name. Nobody will know the difference!

Confetti Crisps

Karen Wilson
Defiance, OH

These simple bars taste like toffee, covered with your favorite candies. They're a favorite cookie that I always include on my Christmas cookie trays. You can substitute your favorite chocolate candies...and how about some colorful sprinkles!

40 saltine crackers
3/4 c. brown sugar, packed
3/4 c. butter
1 t. vanilla extract
1 c. semi-sweet chocolate chips
1 c. mini twist pretzels, broken into small pieces
3/4 c. chocolate-covered crispy peanut butter bars, crushed
3/4 c. chocolate peanut butter cups, chopped
1/2 c. mini candy-coated chocolates

In a lightly greased 15"x10" jelly-roll pan, arrange crackers in a single layer; set aside. Combine brown sugar and butter in a small saucepan. Cook over medium heat, stirring occasionally, until mixture comes to a boil. Boil, stirring constantly, for 4 minutes; stir in vanilla. Pour over crackers and spread evenly. Bake at 350 degrees for 10 to 12 minutes, until hot and bubbly. Remove pan to a wire rack; sprinkle with chocolate chips. Let stand for 3 minutes, allowing chips to soften. Carefully spread melted chocolate over crackers. Sprinkle evenly with remaining ingredients; press gently into chocolate. Let stand at room temperature until set, or refrigerate for 20 to 30 minutes, until chocolate sets up. Cut into squares. Makes 3 to 4 dozen.

Start a journal to note favorite recipes, family preferences, even special guests and celebrations. It's sure to become a cherished keepsake... will make planning special occasions easier too!

Groovy Tie-Dyed Cake

Paula Marchesi
Auburn, PA

This colorful cake is awesome for kids of all ages. It's lots of fun for you and your children to make...they will love to help. Great for family gatherings and parties!

18-1/4-oz. pkg. white cake mix
1-1/2 c. lemon-lime soda
4 to 6 bottles assorted neon food coloring
16-oz. container whipped vanilla frosting
Garnish: candy sprinkles

In a large bowl, combine dry cake mix and soda. Beat with an electric mixer on low speed until well mixed. Reduce speed to medium and beat one more minute. Divide batter among 4 to 6 small bowls. Add 2 to 3 drops food coloring to each bowl; stir until combined. Into a greased and floured 13"x9" baking pan, drop one spoonful of one color of batter. Layer spoonfuls of different colors of batter next to each other, or even on top of the rest of batter. Do not stir! Bake at 350 degrees for 26 to 30 minutes, until a toothpick inserted in the center tests clean. Cool cake in pan on a wire rack; spread with frosting. If desired, frosting may be divided among 3 to 4 bowls and tinted with food coloring. Decorate generously with sprinkles. Serves 12 to 14.

Make canned cake frosting extra special. Scoop it into a bowl and add one teaspoon almond extract. Beat with an electric mixer on medium-high speed until fluffy and double in volume. Simple!

Ice Cream Pies

Marsha Baker
Pioneer, OH

I first tried this yummy recipe after seeing it on a package of cake mix in the early 1970s. Growing up, my kids requested it again & again for birthdays, and they still do! This makes two pies that keep well in the freezer for several weeks...a great make-ahead dessert.

18-oz. devil's food or chocolate fudge cake mix
3/4 c. water
1-1/4 c. chocolate frosting, divided
1/4 c. oil
1/2 gal. favorite ice cream, softened
Optional: chopped peanuts or candies

Generously grease and flour the bottom, sides and rim of two, 9" round cake pans; set aside. In a large bowl, combine dry cake mix, water, 3/4 cup frosting and oil; beat with an electric mixer on high speed for 2 minutes. Spread half of batter in the bottom of each pan; don't spread up the sides. Bake at 350 degrees for 25 to 30 minutes; do not overbake. Centers will be soft when done. Cool completely; cakes will collapse. Spread half of ice cream in each cake shell. Microwave remaining frosting and drizzle over ice cream. Sprinkle with peanuts or candies, if desired. Wrap tightly and freeze at least 2 hours, or up to 2 to 3 weeks. At serving time, allow to stand at room temperature for 10 minutes; cut into wedges. Makes 2 pies; each serves 6 to 8.

Fruit cobblers and crisps can be frozen up to 4 months...bake desserts with ripe summer fruit, then serve them at the holidays! Cool completely, wrap well in plastic wrap and 2 layers of foil. Freeze. To serve, thaw overnight in the fridge, bring to room temperature and rewarm in the oven.

Grandpa Orcutt's Peanut Butter Fudge Sauce

Amber Orcutt-Burke
Russell, PA

When I was growing up, my grandpa used to make this all the time for our family. We served it over ice cream with Spanish peanuts. It has been many years since Grandpa passed away, but this recipe takes me back to being a kid. I can still see him standing at the stove, stirring away. Scrumptious over ice cream...or anything else!

1 c. sugar
2 to 3 t. baking cocoa
1/2 c. milk
1/3 c. margarine
2 T. creamy peanut butter
vanilla extract to taste

Combine sugar, cocoa and milk in a small saucepan. Bring to a boil over medium-high heat; cook for 5 minutes. Turn off heat. Beat in margarine, peanut butter and vanilla. Serve immediately. Makes 4 to 6 servings.

Wet Walnuts Ice Cream Topping

Teresa Verell
Roanoke, VA

My family always has this topping on hand to serve over ice cream...it's awesome!

1 c. white corn syrup
1 c. light brown sugar, packed
3 T. butter
1/2 c. whole milk
1 t. vanilla extract
2 c. chopped walnuts

Combine corn syrup, brown sugar, butter and milk in a saucepan. Bring to a low boil over medium heat, stirring well. Lightly boil for 5 minutes; remove from heat. Add vanilla and walnuts; stir well and allow to cool before serving. Serves 10.

Too much of a good thing is wonderful.

Mae West

Earthquake Cake

Diane Curtis
Dickson, TN

A dear friend shared this recipe with me. It tastes sooo wonderful. When it comes out of the oven, it looks like it has exploded. That's why it's called an Earthquake Cake. But don't worry...it doesn't actually explode, so it won't mess up your oven. The cream cheese mixture, nuts and coconut rise, and it looks really funky. But it tastes delicious!

2/3 c. shredded coconut
2/3 c. semi-sweet chocolate chips
1/2 c. chopped walnuts
18-1/2 oz. pkg. German chocolate cake mix
3 eggs
1-1/3 c. water
1/2 c. oil
8-oz. pkg. cream cheese, softened
1/2 c. butter, softened
2 c. powdered sugar
1 t. vanilla extract
Garnish: frozen whipped topping, thawed

Lightly spray a 13"x9" baking pan with non-stick vegetable spray. Sprinkle coconut, chocolate chips and nuts into pan; set aside. Prepare cake mix according to package directions, using eggs, water and oil. Spread batter over coconut and nuts in pan; set aside. In another bowl, combine cream cheese, butter, powdered sugar and vanilla. Beat until fluffy and spread over batter; gently swirl into batter with a table knife. Bake at 350 degrees for 50 minutes, or until lightly set. Cool; serve topped with whipped topping. Serves 15 to 18.

Make frosted sheet cakes and bar cookies look extra-special. Lightly press a cookie cutter into each frosted square, then use a contrasting tube of frosting to trace the outline.

Can't-Leave-Alone Bars

Meri Hebert
Cheboygan, MI

This is a quick & easy, no-fail treat that we love. Great for potlucks, parties and school snacks. Sometimes I sprinkle flaked coconut or chopped nuts over the chocolate layer before baking. I also use non-stick aluminum foil to line the pan any time I make any bars...makes them easier to cut and no clean-up.

18-1/2 oz. pkg. white cake mix
2 eggs, beaten
1/3 c. oil
1/4 c. margarine
6-oz. pkg. semi-sweet chocolate chips
14-oz. can sweetened condensed milk

In a large bowl, combine dry cake mix, eggs and oil; mix with a fork until blended. Pat half of batter into a greased 13"x9" baking pan; set aside. In a heavy saucepan over low heat, combine margarine, chocolate chips and condensed milk. Cook and stir until melted and smooth; spoon over batter in pan. Top with remaining batter, dropping by spoonfuls. Bake at 350 degrees for 25 to 30 minutes, until golden. Cool; cut into bars. Makes 1-1/2 dozen.

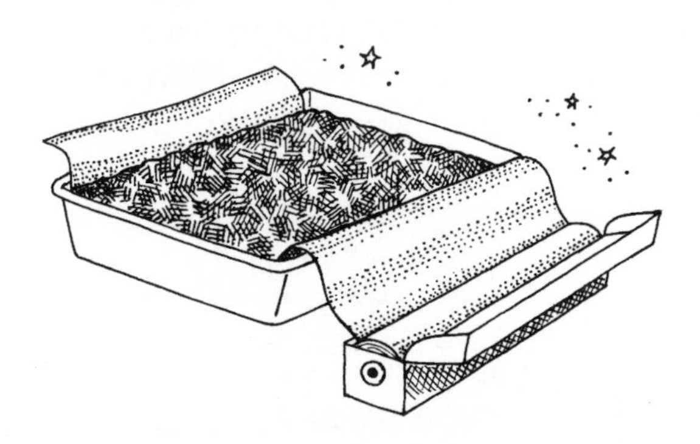

For perfectly cut brownies and bar cookies, line the baking pan with aluminum foil, leaving extra foil for "handles" on either end. After baking, use the foil to lift out the treats onto a cutting board and cut neatly with a long knife.

Festival Pretzel Strawberry Dessert

Nan Calcagno
Grosse Tete, LA

With its gorgeous red color, this old-fashioned dessert has a taste of sweet and salty that you're going to love! Perfect for luncheons and potlucks.

3/4 c. butter, melted
1-1/2 c. sugar, divided
2 c. pretzel twists, crushed and divided
8-oz. pkg. cream cheese, softened
8-oz. container frozen whipped topping, thawed
2 c. pineapple juice
3-oz. pkg. strawberry gelatin mix
10-oz. pkg. frozen sliced strawberries, thawed and drained

In a bowl, combine melted butter, 1/2 cup sugar and 1-1/2 cups crushed pretzels. Mix well; press mixture into the bottom of a lightly greased 13"x9" baking pan, forming a crust. Bake at 350 degrees for 8 minutes; allow to cool. In another bowl, blend together cream cheese, whipped topping and remaining sugar; spread over cooled crust. In a separate bowl, stir together pineapple juice and dry gelatin mix until dissolved; spoon over topping layer. Arrange sliced strawberries on top. Cover and refrigerate until chilled. Cut into squares. Serves 12.

For a family gathering, stir up sweet memories...look through Grandma's recipe box and rediscover a long-forgotten favorite dessert recipe to share.

Cherry Waldorf Gelatin

Cheri Maxwell
Gulf Breeze, FL

My mother has been making this simple dessert for ages. Cool, light and refreshing, it can also double as a salad.

2 c. boiling water
3-oz. pkg. cherry gelatin mix
1 c. cold water
1/4 c. lemon juice
1-1/2 c. Gala apples, peeled, cored and cubed
1 c. celery, diced
1/2 c. chopped walnuts

In a large bowl, combine boiling water and dry gelatin mix. Whisk for about 2 minutes, until dissolved. Stir in cold water and lemon juice; cover and refrigerate until partially set. Fold in apples, celery and nuts. Transfer mixture to a lightly oiled 9"x9" glass baking pan. Cover and chill for 4 to 6 hours, until set. Cut into squares. Makes 8 to 10 servings.

A dollop of fresh whipped cream makes any dessert even more delectable. It's easy, too! Combine one cup whipping cream, 1/4 cup powdered sugar and one teaspoon vanilla extract in a chilled bowl. Beat with chilled beaters until stiff peaks form.

Million-Dollar Pound Cake

Joyce Roebuck
Jacksonville, TX

This is the best pound cake I've ever tasted. It's so versatile. Serve it plain, glazed or topped with fresh fruit and whipped cream. It's always a winner!

1 lb. butter, softened
3 c. sugar
6 eggs, room temperature
4 c. all-purpose flour
3/4 c. milk
1 t. almond extract
1 t. vanilla extract

In a large bowl, with an electric mixer on medium speed, beat together butter and sugar until light and fluffy. Add eggs, one at a time, beating well after each. Gradually add flour alternately with milk, beating well after each addition. Stir in extracts. Pour batter into a well-greased and floured 10" tube pan. Bake at 300 degrees for one hour and 40 minutes, or until cake tests done. Do not open oven door while baking. Cool; turn out onto a cake plate. Makes 16 servings.

Make a luscious sauce for pound cake...simply purée fruit preserves with a few tablespoons of fruit juice. Apricot and strawberry preserves are especially scrumptious. Great for dressing up an angel food cake from the bakery too!

Special-Occasion Desserts

Miracle Chocolate Sauce

Kimberlee Schmidgall
Tremont, IL

My husband's grandmother used to make this ice cream topping. The recipe has been handed down 3 generations so far and remains a staple at family gatherings. Numerous gallons of sauce have been made over the years, as ice cream is our family's most loved treat!

1/2 c. butter
3 sqs. unsweetened baking chocolate
3 c. sugar
12-oz. can evaporated milk
1 t. vanilla extract

Melt butter in a heavy saucepan over medium-low heat. Add chocolate squares; stir until melted. Add sugar and stir; stir in evaporated milk. Bring to a boil; boil for one minute. Remove from heat; stir in vanilla. Cool; cover and refrigerate. May be warmed up in a microwave-safe dish for later use. Makes one quart.

Butterscotch Sauce

Sandy Ann Ward
Anderson, IN

A favorite that Grandma used to make...scrumptious over ice cream and bread pudding.

1/4 c. butter
1 c. brown sugar, packed
1/4 c. whipping cream
1/8 t. salt
1 t. vanilla extract

Melt butter in a heavy saucepan over medium heat. Add brown sugar, cream and salt; stir with a spatula until well mixed. Bring to a boil. Boil for 4 to 5 minutes, scraping down sides of pan occasionally, until thickened and light in color. Remove from heat; stir in vanilla. Cover and refrigerate. Makes about one cup.

Make dessert a grand finale... serve it on your prettiest china!

Blueberry Walnut Squares

Maureen Bordenave
Rio Vista, CA

This is my go-to dessert for get-togethers! It is simple, delicious and such a crowd-pleaser that I'm always asked for the recipe. Everyone from my neighbors to my accountant and her staff has enjoyed it, as well as guests at baby showers, dinner parties and potlucks. For a delicious change, instead of blueberry pie filling, use cherry or lemon. All are excellent...I can't decide which I like the best!

18-1/2 oz. pkg. white cake mix
1-1/4 c. rolled oats, uncooked and divided
1/2 c. butter, softened and divided
1 egg, beaten
21-oz. can blueberry pie filling
1/2 c. chopped walnuts
1/4 c. brown sugar, packed

In a large bowl, combine dry cake mix, one cup oats and 6 tablespoons butter. Mix until crumbly; reserve one cup mixture for topping. To remaining mixture, add egg; mix until well blended. Mixture will be stiff. Press into a greased 13"x9" baking pan. Spoon pie filling over mixture in pan; spread to cover. To reserved crumbs, add remaining oats, remaining butter, walnuts and brown sugar. Mix well; sprinkle over pie filling. Bake at 350 degrees for 35 to 45 minutes, until bubbly and golden. Makes 12 to 16 servings.

Baking bar cookies a few days in advance? They'll stay fresh in their baking pan if tightly covered with aluminum foil.

Nutmeg Feather Cake

Marcia Marcoux
Charlton, MA

Quick & easy! Great with a cup of hot coffee or topped with a scoop of vanilla ice cream. For the best flavor, I like to use freshly ground nutmeg.

1/2 c. butter
1-1/4 c. sugar
1/2 t. vanilla extract
3 eggs, beaten
2 c. all-purpose flour
1 t. baking powder
1 t. baking soda
1/4 t. salt
1 to 2 t. nutmeg
1 c. buttermilk, or 1/2 c. plain yogurt combined with 1/2 c. milk

In a large bowl, blend butter and sugar; stir in vanilla. Add eggs, one at a time, mixing well after each; set aside. In a separate bowl, sift together flour, baking powder, baking soda, salt and nutmeg; add to butter mixture. Stir in buttermilk, a little at a time. Spread batter in a greased and floured 13"x9" baking pan. Bake at 350 degrees for 30 minutes, or until a toothpick inserted in the center comes out clean. Cut into squares. Makes 12 servings.

Make your own flavorful vanilla sugar. Fill a canning jar with 2 cups sugar, push a split vanilla bean into the sugar and let it stand for 2 to 3 weeks. Delicious in hot coffee, or sprinkled over fresh-baked cookies!

Honey Bun Cake

Betty Stewart
Paducah, KY

I received this recipe years ago from my sister-in-law. It's one of those recipes that I've taken to Sunday School over & over again, and it's always a hit!

18-1/2 oz. pkg. yellow cake mix
4 eggs, beaten
8-oz. container sour cream
3/4 c. oil
1/2 c. sugar
3/4 c. light brown sugar, packed
1 T. cinnamon
2-1/2 c. powdered sugar
2 t. vanilla extract
4 to 5 T. milk

In a bowl, combine dry cake mix, eggs, sour cream, oil and sugar. Beat well. Pour half of batter into a greased and floured 13"x9" baking pan; set aside. In another bowl, stir together brown sugar and cinnamon; sprinkle half over batter. Add remaining batter; top with remaining brown sugar mixture. Bake at 275 degrees for 50 to 60 minutes. For glaze, combine powdered sugar, vanilla and enough milk to make a drizzling consistency; drizzle over hot cake. Cut into squares. Serves 20.

Hosting a family reunion? It's a perfect time to update family information. Set out a sign-up sheet and get everyone's phone numbers, e-mail addresses, mailing addresses, children's names, ages and birthdays. Make copies so everyone can stay in touch...you'll be glad you did!

Cheery Cherry Coffee Cake

Marian Forck
Chamois, MO

When we were growing up, my mother always let us pick our birthday cake and I always picked this coffee cake. My siblings were never very pleased, because they didn't think ice cream went with this kind of cake. But, it was my birthday, so Mom would make it for me!

18-1/2 oz. pkg. yellow cake mix
1/4 c. brown sugar, packed
2 T. cinnamon
21-oz. can cherry pie filling
1/4 c. butter, sliced

Prepare cake mix as directed on package. Pour batter into a greased 13"x9" baking pan; set aside. In a cup, combine brown sugar and cinnamon. Drop mixture by spoonfuls over batter in pan; swirl into batter with a table knife. Spoon pie filling over batter; swirl into batter. Scatter butter slices over all. Bake at 350 degrees for 30 minutes. Cut into squares; serve warm. Makes 10 to 12 servings.

Sweet table favors for garden parties and showers! Pick a mini spring bouquet and place in a jelly jar...attach a leaf-shaped tag with the guest's name on it.

Brownie Bottom Cheesecake Squares

Sandra Mirando
Depew, NY

My Aunt Mary and I used to make these brownies all the time. We love them and they are so easy.

18-1/2 oz. pkg. devil's food cake mix
1/2 c. butter
3 eggs, divided
2 8-oz. pkgs. cream cheese, softened
3/4 c. sugar

In a large bowl, combine dry cake mix, butter and one egg; blend well. Press mixture into the bottom of a greased 13"x9" baking pan; set aside. In another bowl, combine remaining eggs, cream cheese and sugar. Beat until smooth and well blended; spoon over batter in pan. Bake at 325 degrees for 40 to 45 minutes, until edges are very lightly golden. Cool; ice with Chocolate Frosting and cut into squares. Makes 2 dozen.

Chocolate Frosting:

6-oz. pkg. semi-sweet chocolate chips
8-oz. container sour cream

Combine chocolate chips and sour cream in a saucepan. Cook over low heat, stirring constantly, until chocolate melts and mixture is smooth. Remove from heat; cool until just warm.

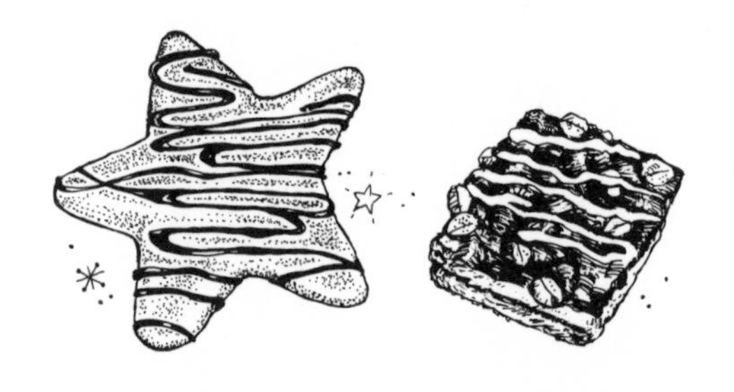

A drizzle of melted white chocolate makes a chocolate dessert extra special.

Grandma Cora's Cream Puff Cake

Leona Krivda
Belle Vernon, PA

I always loved it when my grandma made this dessert, it is so yummy! And now when I make it, my family loves it also. So happy to be sharing my special recipes with my family.

1 c. water
1/2 c. butter, softened
1 c. all-purpose flour
4 eggs
8-oz. pkg. cream cheese, softened
3-1/2 c. milk
2 3.4-oz. pkgs. instant vanilla pudding mix
8-oz. container frozen whipped topping, thawed
Garnish: chocolate syrup
Optional: chopped nuts

Combine water and butter in a saucepan over medium-high heat; bring to a boil. Add flour all at once and stir till very well mixed. Remove from heat; cool for 2 minutes. Add eggs, one at a time, beating well after each. Spread batter in a well-greased 13"x9" baking pan. Bake at 450 degrees for 15 minutes. Turn oven to 350 degrees; bake for another 20 to 25 minutes. Cool completely in pan. In a large bowl, beat cream cheese with an electric mixer on medium speed until smooth. Slowly beat in milk and dry pudding mixes; spoon over cooled crust. Spread whipped topping over all. Drizzle with chocolate syrup and sprinkle with nuts, if desired. Cover with plastic wrap; keep refrigerated. Serves 12 to 15.

It can be really tricky to double or triple recipe ingredients for baked goods. For the best results, choose a recipe that feeds a bunch, or prepare several batches of a single recipe until you have the quantity you need.

Pineapple Angel Food Dessert

Taylor Bielski
Wethersfield, CT

This is a family favorite that I've been making since my sons were young...they are now adults with families of their own. I still make it for family gatherings. For the Fourth of July, I like to use strawberries & blueberries for the red, white and blue.

1 angel food cake, broken into chunks
8-oz. pkg. cream cheese, softened
3 c. milk
2 3-oz. pkgs. instant vanilla pudding mix
15-1/4 oz. can crushed pineapple, well drained
8-oz. container frozen whipped topping, thawed
Optional: chopped walnuts, cherries, blueberries

Spread cake chunks in an ungreased 13"x9" glass baking pan; set aside. In a large bowl, beat cream cheese with an electric mixer on medium speed until smooth. Gradually beat in milk until smooth. Add dry pudding mix and stir until starting to thicken; spoon over cake chunks. Spread pineapple over cream cheese mixture. Spread whipped topping over pineapple. Cover and refrigerate if not serving immediately. Garnish as desired; cut into squares. Makes 12 servings.

To keep a chilled dessert cool on a warm day, just fill a picnic basket with plastic zipping bags full of ice, lay a colorful tablecloth over the ice and set the sweets on top.

Strawberry Party Cake

Sally Jo Lowry
Urbana, OH

This good old-fashioned poke cake is easy and scrumptious. Use different kinds of berries for a different delicious flavor every time.

18-1/2 oz. pkg. white cake mix
14-oz. can sweetened condensed milk
8-oz. pkg. cream cheese, softened
1 lb. fresh strawberries, hulled and sliced
8-oz. container frozen whipped topping, thawed

Prepare and bake cake mix as directed on package, using a greased 13"x9" baking pan. Cool; use a wooden spoon handle or fork to poke 16 holes in the top of cooled cake. In a blender, combine condensed milk, cream cheese and strawberries; process until well blended. Pour milk mixture into the holes and over the top of cake. Cover and refrigerate for 3 hours, or until set. At serving time, spread whipped topping over cake. Cut into squares. Makes 12 to 16 servings.

To make any cake mix extra rich and moist, add one more egg than called for in the package directions.

Super-Soft Sugar Cookies

Hollie Moots
Marysville, OH

I've been making these cookies for years and they are always a hit! They're so soft...the perfect base for your favorite frosting, with sprinkles to match the occasion.

1 c. butter, softened
1 c. sugar
2 whole eggs
3 egg yolks
1 t. vanilla extract
3-1/2 c. all-purpose flour
1-1/2 t. baking powder
1/4 t. salt
Garnish: frosting, candy sprinkles

In a large bowl, blend butter and sugar until pale. Beat in eggs and egg yolks, one at a time, mixing well after each addition. Add vanilla; set aside. In another bowl, combine flour, baking powder and salt; stir into butter mixture. Cover and chill dough for at least one hour. Roll out dough on a floured surface, 1/4 to 1/2 inch thick. Cut with favorite cookie cutters and place on parchment paper-lined baking sheets. Bake at 375 degrees for 8 to 10 minutes, just until golden, depending on size of cookies. Cool for 2 to 3 minutes on baking sheets; remove to a wire rack to cool. Decorate with frosting and sprinkles, as desired. Makes 3 dozen.

Cookie cutters come in so many shapes, you're sure to find some to match any theme! Heap on the frosting and sprinkles to serve for dessert, or wrap in cellophane for yummy take-home favors.

Chocolate-Peanut Butter Cookie Pizza

Linda McCullough
Clearwater, KS

Our family enjoys this fun dessert and it is very easy to make. Originally, a friend brought it to a lunch gathering where I work, and we have been making it ever since!

16-1/2 oz. pkg. refrigerated chocolate chip cookie dough
8-oz. pkg. cream cheese, softened
1/2 c. creamy peanut butter
1/4 c. milk
1 c. powdered sugar
1 c. frozen whipped topping, thawed
3/4 c. hot fudge topping, divided
1/4 c. chopped peanuts

Break up cookie dough onto an ungreased 12" round pizza pan. With floured hands, press dough evenly into bottom of pan, forming a crust. Bake at 350 degrees for 15 to 20 minutes, until golden. Cool completely, about 30 minutes. Meanwhile, in a large bowl, combine cream cheese, peanut butter, milk and powdered sugar; beat until smooth. Fold in whipped topping; set aside. Spread 1/2 cup fudge topping over cooled crust; spread peanut butter mixture over top. Drizzle with remaining fudge topping; sprinkle with peanuts. Cover and refrigerate for at least 30 minutes, until serving time. Cut into wedges or squares. Serves 8 to 10.

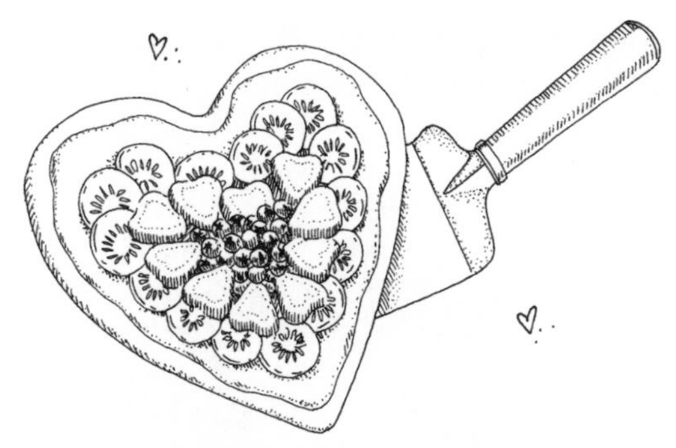

Everyone loves a dessert pizza! For another way with a sugar cookie crust, blend an 8-ounce package cream cheese, 1/2 cup sugar and one teaspoon vanilla; spread over cooled crust. Arrange sliced fresh fruit over crust and cut into wedges. Yummy!

Chocolate-Cherry Tea Cakes

Irene Putman
Canal Fulton, OH

Love, love, love these cookies! They're different from regular tea cakes and are always a hit with chocolate lovers. Great for holiday cookie exchanges, because no one else will have the same cookie as you... they'll all want the recipe. Scrumptious!

1 c. butter, softened
1 c. powdered sugar
2-1/4 c. all-purpose flour
2 sqs. semi-sweet baking chocolate, melted
1/4 t. salt
3/4 c. maraschino cherries, drained and chopped

In a large bowl, blend together butter and powdered sugar. Stir in flour, melted chocolate and salt; blend well. Fold in cherries. Roll dough into one-inch balls. Arrange on ungreased cookie sheets, one inch apart. Bake at 350 degrees for 12 to 16 minutes. Immediately remove cookies to a wire rack and cool. Drizzle Glaze over cooled cookies. Makes 4 to 5 dozen.

Glaze:

3/4 c. powdered sugar
1 sq. semi-sweet baking chocolate, melted
1 T. butter, softened

Combine all ingredients in a bowl; blend until smooth. You may want to double glaze recipe if you like a lot of sweet glaze on your cookies.

Spend a free morning baking up a batch of a favorite cookie treat, then invite a special friend in for an impromptu cookie tea time.

Blushing Cookie Triangles

Erin Brock
Charleston, WV

This recipe makes lots of cookies...great for a brunch table or cookie trays. I like to use several different jams for variety.

1 c. butter, softened
8-oz. pkg. cream cheese, softened
2 c. all-purpose flour
1 t. salt
2/3 c. favorite jam or preserves
Garnish: powdered sugar or glaze

Combine butter and cream cheese in a large bowl. Beat with an electric mixer on medium speed until blended and smooth. In a separate bowl, mix flour and salt. Add to butter mixture; stir until well blended. Divide dough evenly into 3 balls. Cover and chill for one hour. On a floured surface, roll out each ball into a 15-inch by 7-1/2 inch rectangle. Cut each rectangle into 18 squares, 2-1/2 inches each. Drop 1/2 teaspoon jam in the center of each square; fold over to form a triangle. Place on ungreased baking sheets. Bake at 350 degrees for 15 minutes, or until lightly golden. Cool cookies on wire racks; sprinkle with powdered sugar or drizzle with glaze. Makes about 4-1/2 dozen.

Parchment paper is a baker's best friend! Place it on a baking sheet to keep cookies from spreading and sticking. It can usually be reused at least once, too. When it starts to darken and dry out, just toss it.

INDEX

Beverages

Breads & Crackers

Breakfast & Brunch

Condiments

Cookies

Crunchy Treats & Nuts

Dessert Toppings

Desserts

INDEX

Dips & Spreads

Finger Foods

Main Dishes

INDEX

Salads & Slaws

Sandwiches

Side Dishes

Soups & Stews